CAPTAIN SALLY

A Biography of Capt. Sally Tompkins, America's First Female Army Officer

THOMAS T. WIATT

ISBN: 978-1-4834-9359-6 (sc)
ISBN: 978-1-4834-9358-9 (e)

Because of the dynamic nature of the Internet, any web addresses or
links contained in this book may have changed since publication and
may no longer be valid. The views expressed in this work are solely those
of the author and do not necessarily reflect the views of the publisher,
and the publisher hereby disclaims any responsibility for them.

This book is a work of non-fiction. Unless otherwise noted, the author
and the publisher make no explicit guarantees as to the accuracy of
the information contained in this book and in some cases, names of
people and places have been altered to protect their privacy.

Any people depicted in stock imagery provided by Getty Images are
models, and such images are being used for illustrative purposes only.
Certain stock imagery © Getty Images.

Scripture taken from the King James Version of the Bible.

Lulu Publishing Services rev. date: 11/13/2018

Sally Louisa Tompkins c. 1860's.
The American Civil War Museum,
under the management of
the Virginia Museum of History and Culture

"What I did for the wounded and ill Confederate soldiers was entirely a work of love"

– Sally Louisa Tompkins 1907

CONTENTS

ACKNOWLEDGEMENTS

A very special thanks go out to Becky Foster Barnhardt of the Mathews County Historical Society's archives, located at the Mathews Memorial Library, in Mathews, Virginia. Her help was invaluable in putting me in touch with so much research and information.

Thanks to Beth DeHardit Richardson of Gloucester County Glo-Quips newspaper for being supportive and for putting me in touch with editor Fran Musick, also my sister Laura Wiatt Beavers and Herbert Greene, who also helped with the editing.

The Virginia Museum of History and Culture and the Library of Virginia in Richmond, Virginia deserve a shout out for allowing me access to their photo collection and St. James's Church in Richmond, Virginia for granted me permission for the use the photograph of their stained glass image of Capt. Sally Tompkins.

Thanks to Sara Hunt of the Virginia Woman's Monument Commission for her help.

My brother Alexander Lloyd Wiatt gets a special thanks for bringing the Sally Tompkins story to my attention and for helping with the research.

FOREWORD

Sally Tompkins' birthplace, Poplar Grove, is only about thirty some miles from my home in Newport News, Virginia. Even so, I knew very little about Sally Tompkins except that her name would sometimes pop up in books about the American Civil War or from local historical markers like the ones in Mathews, Virginia. Her name even showed up in my great-great grandfather's Civil War journal. He was the chaplain of the Twenty-sixth Virginia Infantry and he sent Sally twenty dollars that he had collected from the men.

When I finally set out to write this book, I was delighted to find, through my research, that Sally and I are third cousins thrice removed through the Todd family and a second cousin four times removed through the Field family.

I think this woman's ability to do the impossible, and do it for years under the worst conditions, makes her the ideal American.

Thomas T. Wiatt 2019

INTRODUCTION

S ally Tompkins was not a particularly attractive woman, plain by most accounts.[1] She seldom smiled and was always plainly dressed. In spite of her appearance, she was adored by the Confederate troops and received probably hundreds of marriage proposals, all of which she declined. It was said that "her strength of mind and character took the place of more frivolous charms."[2]

She was called many things such as "The Lady with the milk-white hands," "The Angel of the Confederacy" and even "Dearest of Captains." The troops mostly just called her "Captain Sally."

She was a nurse who owned and ran her own private hospital in Richmond, Virginia during the American Civil War. The hospital had the highest survival rate of any hospital north or south. This statistic was even more remarkable considering that the worst cases were sent to her.

She was also commissioned as Captain in the Confederate Cavalry because, by law, all hospitals had to be under military rule to be able to receive medical supplies.

Her commission was unprecedented and unique in the American military until women were eligible to be Army officers in the Army Nurse Corps in 1901. Prior to the establishment of the Women's Army Auxiliary Corps in World War II, federal authorities procured and studied copies of her commission.

This five-foot-tall woman could work tirelessly and as hard as any man. More importantly, Sally Tompkins demonstrated that women were capable of doing so many things that, in this time period, women were thought incapable of doing. As a hospital administrator, she challenged gender expectations and helped to expand the role of women in all management positions.

Poplar Grove
The Library of Virginia

CHAPTER 1

Poplar Grove

P oplar Grove is a handsome estate near the Tidewater community of Williams in rural Mathews County, Virginia. On the estate sits an eighteenth-century mansion overlooking large oaks, magnolia and poplar trees, and a sweeping lawn of lush grass and daffodils that slopes down to the East River. The central portion of the house is a late eighteenth-century temple-form building fronted by a columned portico. A part of a serpentine brick wall still remains. The atmosphere is very quiet. Often deer, quail and bluebirds make the only sounds a visitor will hear.

The property contains one of the few historic tide mills left in the country. It was originally built in colonial times, but was burned down by Union troops during the American Civil War. The present mill was built shortly after the war and remained operational until 1912. The tide mill is a two-story frame structure with a gable roof built on a narrow channel which separates a mill pond from the East River near the Chesapeake Bay.

The earliest known owner of the property was Samuel Williams. Tax records show that Colonel John Patterson[3] owned a home there in 1795. Having served in the American Revolutionary War, Patterson became a prominent member of the Mathews community and served as a member of the Virginia State

Legislature[4]. Patterson's daughter, Mariah[5] (she went by Maria), married Colonel Christopher Tompkins in 1815, and Tompkins acquired the house and property at his father-in-law's death in 1824.

The Tompkins family came from ancient lineage, tracing their roots back to Thom the Saxon who most likely came to England with William the Conqueror during the Norman Conquest of 1066[6]. Christopher's ancestor, Humphrey Tompkins, came to Virginia from England (probably in the mid 17th century) and settled on the York River in Gloucester County.

Colonel Christopher Tompkins, a War of 1812 veteran, had come to nearby Mathews County in 1804 to supervise the construction of ships and became a very wealthy trade agent in the West Indies and in Europe. He had eight children, four from a previous marriage (only three survived[7]) and four with Maria. Also living at Poplar Grove was their second cousin (from Maria's side) Harriet Ann Field who had been orphaned at the age of four in 1826. Sally Louisa Tompkins was the youngest of Maria's children, having been born in 1833.

The plantation grew its own cotton which was spun and woven into bedspreads and tablecloths and beautifully embroidered by Maria Tompkins. Even as a small child Sally liked being helpful and would even beg to be allowed to make some of the ornamental stitches.

It was a lively household then with parties and dances. Colonel Tompkins and his wife Maria would invite many friends and even the older Tompkins children would join in the festivities. Everyone would be dressed in their finest clothes. Slaves would provide the music on fiddles for the Virginia Reel as young Sally would watch from the top of the stairs. Food would include Virginia ham, fried chicken, a variety of fruits and vegetables, oysters, pudding and blackberry pies.

Sadly the joy of the household ended when Colonel Christopher Tompkins became very ill in late 1837. His wife Maria wrote of his sickness[8]:

> Mr. Thompkins' health for the last fortnight has
> been still worse - he has taken cold and had a
> great many returns of the asthma in very quick
> secretion he suffered as much last week that [sic]
> on Saturday... as soon as he got here Cousin Henry
> bled him, but his shortness of breath and cough was
> not relieved... Dr. Dabney who as soon as he came
> put a large plaster on his side and gave him flaxseed
> tea & tartar water to drink – he spent as bad a night
> last night as he has done for several nights past ....

The bleeding (or bloodletting) referred to in Maria's letter was an ancient system of medical treatment already dying out in America (and most of the world) by this time in the nineteenth century. Although it was successful in temporarily reducing blood pressure, which resulted in some relief to the patient, it also weakened the sick and usually did more harm than good. This type of primitive medical treatment may have contributed to Colonel Tompkins' death the next year. His short obituary, published in a Richmond, Virginia paper, spoke volumes about the character of the man:

> Few private gentlemen filled more space in the eyes
> of the community; and the death of no man in his
> county will produce a greater chasm. Col. Tompkins
> was the artificer of his own fortune: from indigence
> and obscurity, he went forth into the world a
> friendless boy, and by the force and power of a
> well-regulated mind and industry that never slept,
> he acquired wealth, standing and consequence in
> society.[9]

When Colonel Tompkins died in 1838, Sally was not quite five years old. Her oldest half-brother Christopher, Jr. was serving in the military at the time of his father's death and that fact left her twenty-year-old brother, Benjamin, to manage the farm. Even with her father's death, life went on as usual at Poplar Grove.

Sally was particularly close to her older sister Elizabeth (called Lizzy) although she was seventeen years Sally's senior. She saw her older sister as a mentor and role model. Elizabeth was a very shy person but an intensely religious one. Her religious fervor led her to be associated with the American Colonization Society. The society believed that slaves would face better chances for freedom and prosperity in Africa than in America. The society supported the migration of free African Americans to the African country of Liberia. Elizabeth freed her own personal slaves and sent them to Liberia, although some were very reluctant to go.

All the Tompkins children had been baptized in Ware Parish Episcopal Church near the town of Gloucester Court House, Virginia in neighboring Gloucester County, Virginia. The whole family were steady churchgoers but Ware Parish seemed like a long carriage ride since they passed the ruins of an old abandoned Episcopal church each Sunday on their way to Ware church. This church was built in 1690 and had been called the Kingston Parish Church.

Elizabeth also took it upon herself to rebuild the Kingston Parish Church (now called Christ Church) that was very close to Poplar Grove. Elizabeth oversaw the rebuilding of the church and solicited the funds necessary until its completion in 1841. A priest was soon hired and it became an active church that was also conveniently nearby.

In all probability, Sally's cousin and adopted sister, Harriet Field, left Poplar Grove when she married John Lightfoot in 1841. Harriet and John had a home in Port Royal, Virginia. She may have left the area just in time.

The tragedy of the yellow fever epidemic that swept through the South in 1842 shook the Tompkins family to its very foundation. Sally's beloved sister, Elizabeth Tompkins, became the first to become ill and died suddenly on September 2, 1842. Her oldest sister, Martha, took ill and died shortly after Elizabeth's funeral on September 17, 1842. Martha's husband, Dr. Henry Wythe Tabb, wrote of her death:

> ...my wife was attacked by a bilious remittent fever, which proved obstinate but after a time was apparently subdued; some little imprudence brought on a relapse and she died in a chill. All means internal and external failing to restore the circulation. She died without a struggle, in the full possession of all her faculties.[10]

Her next oldest sister, Harriet, who had nursed Martha, died of the same disease just a few days later on September 20, 1842. Although she was only a child of nine years, Sally was thrust into helping with the nursing and care of her dying sisters. One of the Tompkins' eighty some slaves was a cook named Phoebe who was said to be a quite efficient nurse herself.[11] Sally most likely received much of her early nursing education from her.

Sally's half-brother, Christopher, Jr., had graduated from the College of William and Mary at only seventeen years of age and West Point at twenty three. He had made the military his life and was sent first to Texas then to California during the War with Mexico in 1845-46. Although the conquest of California had been completed by the time he got there, Sally was extremely proud of him and his military service. She wrote to him:

> My dearest brother,
>
> You cannot imagine the deep regret that we all felt on receiving the news of your intended departure for Texas and the sympathy for dear sister Ellen's [Christopher's wife] distress which no doubt was very great. I hope you will be able to distinguish yourself in the battle and be a second George Washington and come home to receive congratulations from all of your friends. Then how glad we should feel and how

proud mama and sister Ellen would be to hear your praises sounded by everyone when Joe [Christopher's son] and the baby grow up to hear the exploits of their father and copy after them. Sister Ellen must certainly come down and stay with Ma while you are gone. I am sure we will anticipate every wish of her heart and will soon prevent her from missing you all. Brother Ben is ready to go so I will have to bid you good bye. May you be protected from all danger is the sincere prayer of your devoted sister.[12]

It had been only five years since the loss of three of her sisters, and not quite fourteen-year-old Sally had to deal with another unexpected illness in the family. Her twenty-eight-year old half-brother, Benjamin Tompkins, became ill with Tuberculosis in 1847.

With few available doctors, the women in a plantation family were usually the primary caregivers. The Tompkins women were not only responsible for the care of the family but also for the care of the many slaves. Some legends from undocumented sources state that Sally learned much of her nursing skills from practicing nursing on a playmate (and slave) known as Caroline Matilda Brown.[13] The family cook, Phoebe, may have taught Sally how to make a salve from boiling sassafras roots. She was said to have learned many healing remedies from an elderly slave called "Uncle Solomon."[14]

With fewer womenfolk left in the family during Benjamin's illness, Sally had to play a much larger role in his nursing than she had with her sisters years earlier.

Benjamin soon died of his sickness and his death was certainly devastating to Sally. He had been more of a father to her than a brother. His Richmond, Virginia newspaper obituary stated, "youngest son of the late Colonel Christopher Tompkins, and like his lamented father, bade fair to become one of our most useful and respected citizens." Benjamin was the last male family member left to run Poplar Grove, and it would be difficult for the remaining ladies to run the estate on their own. Some decisions needed to be made.

Sally Louisa Tompkins c. 1850's.
The American Civil War Museum,
under the management of
the Virginia Museum of History and Culture

CHAPTER 2

Antebellum Richmond

With Benjamin gone and Christopher Tompkins, Jr. being away in the military, there was no male family member left to run the estate. With Christopher's blessing, Sally's mother reluctantly sold the family estate, Poplar Grove, in 1849. The loss of her childhood home devastated Sally, but her mother felt that they had little choice.

After selling Poplar Grove, Maria Tompkins and her two remaining children, Sally and Maria Mason, soon moved near Norfolk, Virginia to start a new life. Accompanying them were eight of the family slaves, including Churchill the coachman, Phoebe the cook, Peter Smith, "Sad" Betsey Curtis and "Glad" Betsey Ashberry and possibly Caroline Matilda Brown and Uncle Solomon. They all lived at #52 West Freemason Street,[15] which in those days was considered "out in the country," although only a mile from the small town of Norfolk.

When the family was still at Poplar Grove, Maria Tompkins had hired a governess to tutor her two remaining children.[16] Now in Norfolk, the girls enrolled in the Norfolk Female Institute where they studied "Classical English and polite education." This was a new school affiliated with the Episcopal Church. They finished their studies in 1850 and it is unknown if they ever furthered their education. There is no indication that they did, although they were said to be very bright children.

In January 1854, Sally, her mother, sister Maria and their slave Phoebe (and perhaps others) moved to Richmond, Virginia. Although Richmond had been the capital city of Virginia since 1781, it was really just a small quiet city of about 38,000[17] souls by 1860. Many of its brick buildings dated back to the colonial period.

Richmond was more industrialized than most Southern cities. The Industrial Revolution arrived in the city beginning in the 1830s with the addition of railroads and foundries. Being a centrally located city on the James River at the fall line, Richmond became the center of regional communications. The city housed several newspapers, book publishers and colleges all helping shape public opinion and further the education of the populace.

Since the Tompkins family had done business in Richmond for many years, they were welcomed with open arms. They rented rooms in a boarding house in the city called the Arlington House owned by Macy C. Morton.[18] Unfortunately, mother Maria became ill almost as soon as they moved in. Her ribs were constricted with pleurisy.[19] They did what they could to make her comfortable, but she died only a few months after their arrival. Sally, her sister Maria and Phoebe were heartbroken. Their mother was taken back to Poplar Grove and was buried there. For the rest of her life, Sally kept a lock of her mother's hair inside a brooch, with her mother's photograph on the other side. An inscription read "My Mother / March 29, 1854."

Brother Christopher Tompkins visited his half-sisters in Richmond soon after their mother died. He owned a mountaintop plantation in what is now West Virginia and wanted them to move there. He did not think that Sally and Maria should live alone in the city. The girls were 27 (Maria) and 24 (Sally) years old and felt they were old enough to live wherever they wished. They wished to stay in Richmond, and they did.

While living in Richmond, Sally was active at St. James Church teaching Sunday School. She was a devoted Episcopalian. She sewed for the poor and continued to nurse sick relatives and friends.

In 1850's Richmond, Sally and Maria did have somewhat of a social life. They received many invitations to dances, parties, teas and the like. Girlhood, at this time in the South, consisted of a series of "rites of passage" through which girls progressed their way to womanhood. Events like parties, dances and debuts were the norm for young women of their status. The recent deaths in the family most likely had distracted and diverted her mother's attention away from introducing Sally and her sister into Virginia society. Except for a brief flirtation with a young man named Edmund at the Cherry Hill, Virginia home of their friends the Taylors, Sally probably experienced no youthful romantic involvement.[20]

Although Sally was never known to have any romantic relationships, she certainly seemed to have her share of male friends. One may have been William Robb, who enjoyed ice skating when the James River froze in the winter. Ice skating had become a "craze" since the 1840s, but at that time it was a "men only event" and considered not very "ladylike." Women would sit in chairs on the ice and the men would push them around as William did for Sally.[21]

Another male friend of Sally's was Walter H. Taylor. He was 'an attorney in Richmond and handled all of Sally Tompkins' financial affairs. She often addressed him as "My Dear Walter." One man whom Sally thought a great deal of was the Reverend Joshua Peterson who presided over St. James Church in Richmond where Sally attended. He was more like a father figure to her. She wrote of him, "our dear pastor…[I] have looked to him more than any other human being for counsel and comfort."[22]

Life was good for what was left of the Tompkins family during this period. It would not last. This time of their lives could be described as "the calm before the storm."

Richmond, Virginia before the Civil War
U.S. Nation Archives

CHAPTER 3

The Gathering Storm

The United States had become increasingly divided during the 1850s over sectional disagreements, especially regarding the extension of slavery into new states being created from the western territories. In 1860, the Republican Party was a new political party replacing the Whig Party as the major opposition to the Democrats. Its leader was Abraham Lincoln who had opposed the further extension of slavery into the territories. It had been well known that Lincoln personally opposed the institution of slavery. Secession and war were in the minds of many and seemed to be the subject of every conversation all over Richmond and the South.

The Democratic Party was split between two candidates, Douglas who felt that each individual territory had the right to decide its status of slavery and Breckinridge who was proslavery.

A fourth political party emerged, and that was the Constitutional Union Party with John Bell as its leader. Bell wanted simply to avoid the slavery question and also was opposed to secession. Virginia, as well as the other border states, overwhelmingly supported Bell for the presidency. One might assume that Sally did too, but no one knows for certain. There are no known records of Sally ever speaking of or expressing her opinion about politics except after the war started when she was known to be very pro-Confederate.

By 1860, Sally and sister Maria had moved to a large boarding house called The Arlington House on the corner of Sixth and Main. Because of the pending War, Maria soon moved to Port Royal in northeastern Virginia near their cousin and adopted sister Harriet Field Lightfoot. Sally stayed in Richmond to become a close eyewitness to the War's horrors.[23]

The election of Lincoln led to the secession of several states in the South, and war seemed inevitable. A nation called "The Confederate States of America" was formed and a constitution was written. Jefferson Davis was named its President. The capital of this new nation was Montgomery, Alabama.

Hostilities began on April 12, 1861, when Confederate forces fired on the Union-occupied Fort Sumter, in Charleston, South Carolina. This event helped unify the North and caused anger toward the Southern states. At this moment Virginia and the border states were not a part of the Confederacy. Virginia had hoped to avoid secession and a war, but U.S. President Lincoln's call upon Virginia to supply troops to put down the rebellion forced Virginia to choose sides. Virginia joined the Confederacy on April 17, 1861, and the powers that be decided that the capital would be moved to Richmond. This placed Sally Tompkins into the thick of it.

Although no great or notable battles were fought for the first few months, there were small skirmishes against Union troops nearly everywhere. Many of these were organized by men who were more like pro-secession mobs than real armies. There were riots in Baltimore, Maryland against Union troops, and small battles at Big Bethel near Hampton, Virginia, at the town of Philippi in West Virginia and at Fairfax Court House, Virginia. None of these could be considered battles by later Civil War standards and had little to no effect on life in Richmond Virginia.

In the meantime, the Southern states were trying to organize a country and a military. On the morning of May 30, 1861, President Jefferson Davis arrived in Richmond. As the capital of the

Confederacy, Richmond was not only the seat of the Confederate Government but also served as the capital of Virginia as well. Most of the available government buildings were over occupied and crowded. Since no real fighting had happened yet, the coming flood of thousands of wounded and sick soldiers could not even be imagined by the city's citizens. They were completely unprepared for what was to come.

Wounded men being brought into Richmond.
Sketch by William Ludwell Sheppard

CHAPTER 4

Real War Begins

The first major battle of the American Civil War was the battle of Bull Run in July 1861, and there would be many more. What led up to this battle was the attempt by Union troops to capture Richmond with an army of 35,000 poorly trained men. The Confederates had a force of about 32,000 engaged to defend their Capital. Bull Run was a small river near the town of Manassas, Virginia about 90 miles north of Richmond, but much closer to Washington, DC. It was a clash of amateur armies. Although the battle was a southern victory, the cost was very high. There were approximately 1900 wounded and 500 killed just on the Confederate side on that hot summer day in July.

To use the modern day vernacular, the War hit the South and even more so Richmond, "like a ton of bricks." No one had any idea that the War would be so large and last for so long. Richmond was completely unprepared for the large number of wounded troops that poured into the city.

What partly contributed to the high casualty rate was the fact that the troops (on both sides) were untrained in battle tactics. There was confusion everywhere. Uniforms varied in color. Flags were not recognized. Some soldiers were just ignorant about how to form battle formations. Some, mistakenly, even fired on their own fellow soldiers. In spite of all this confusion, the Confederates managed to force the Union troops away from Richmond. Sally, at first, was excited about the news of the victory perhaps not knowing the cost. Shortly after she wrote of this to her sister Maria:

> This afternoon Mrs. Lee [General Robert E. Lee's sister-in-law] told me that the battle had begun at four o'clock and oh the intense anxiety we all felt, for it must be a struggle, bloody and terrible...I felt constrained to go to church tonight to join my poor prayers with the people for victory and surely we all prayed from our inmost souls...When I got to Arlington [Sally's boarding house] I saw the dispatch which Gen. Cooper received. It read thus: 'Night is closing in – we have won a glorious but dearly bought victory, The day and the field are ours - the enemy are [sic] in full flight – all my forces in close pursuit. Jefferson Davis.' I felt that we could indeed say 'thy right hand, O Lord, is become glorious in power, thy right hand, O Lord, hath dashed in pieces the enemy.' Read the lesson today, the 8th Sunday of the Trinity, and see how applicable they are to us now.[24]

The number of wounded soldiers was astounding to the citizens of Richmond. Long lines of ambulances slowly toiled into the city, filled with wounded being carried to various city hospitals. Trails of blood from the wounded could be seen on the city streets, along with wagonloads of dead piled one upon the other. This sight moved Sally as it would have anyone.

The atmosphere of Richmond completely changed due to the war. The once quiet city of 38,000 would swell to 128,000 by the war's end, which put a strain on food supplies. The increase in male population brought prostitution, drinking, gambling, street fights, and even cockfighting dens.

The newly formed Confederate government called upon the

citizens of the city to care for the sick and wounded returning from battle. The citizens responded in any way they were able. Many hospitals sprung up, mostly military ones, like Chimborazo Hospital which was the largest in the world with 5,000 beds.

Sally took it upon herself to do the nearly impossible. She wanted to start her own hospital and supply it using her own money. Fortunately for many wounded soldiers, Sally had connections. A very good friend of her late father, Judge John Robertson, chose to leave Richmond and flee to a remote farm in western Virginia for the duration of the war. This left the Robertson's large home on the corner of Third and Main vacant. Conveniently, the Robertson home was only three blocks away from Sally's boarding house. Judge Robertson agreed to let twenty-seven year old Sally use his home as a hospital during his family's absence. It would be known as the Robertson Hospital.

Some of the female social elite of Richmond rallied to assist Miss Sally. They had all the furniture moved upstairs to make room for beds on the first floor. When Mrs. Robertson learned of this exclusion she insisted that the furniture be used for the hospital thus increasing the bed space.[25] The hospital was up and running only ten days after the battle. Robertson Hospital received its first patient on August 1, 1861, only one day after opening for business.

With supplies sometimes not available, corn leaves were used as bandages. At times the only medicine was whiskey and turpentine. In spite of its hardships, it quickly became apparent that Sally's hospital had the highest percentage [about 95%] of patient recovery of any hospital, North or South. Sally attributed her success to "the best nursing and perfect cleanliness." Providing the sick with fresh fruit and vegetables grown locally on the hospital grounds was certainly also a factor. Since the principle of germ theory didn't receive any attention until the late 1850's due to Louis Pasteur's work, it is very doubtful that she had any scientific basis for her belief that cleanliness attributed to her hospital's success rate. It was probably just a hunch, perhaps based only on her observations. The same might be said for her providing fresh fruit and vegetables since little was known of nutrition at that time. Hunch or not, she was absolutely correct.

Much credit for the success of Sally's Robertson Hospital went to the top notch staff she personally hired. Her large staff included many nurses and doctors, cooks, gardeners, carpenters and even blockade runners who brought her supplies. She also had a large number of paid slaves and "free men of color" in her employ.

Sally first brought to the hospital some of her personal slaves including Phoebe, who had helped raise Sally since the time when she was a baby. There was also Betsy Curtis and Betsy Ashberry (known as "Sad Betsy" and "Glad Betsy," respectively, nicknames that were given to them by the patients)[26] and two others named Peter Smith and Churchill.

Sally hired several doctors to assist her, including Dr. Alexander Yelverton Peyron Garnett (known as Dr. A.Y.P. Garnett) as her head surgeon. Dr. Garnett was thought to be one of the best doctors in the land. He was originally from Essex County, Virginia but he began studying medicine at the University of Pennsylvania. After graduation, he was appointed Assistant Surgeon in the Navy. He was stationed at Washington D.C., but later resigned his position in the Navy and began his career as a civilian physician. He was then elected to the chair of Theory and Practice of Medicine in the National Medical College of Columbia University (now George Washington University School of Medicine & Health Sciences and one of the most prestigious medical research schools in the U.S.).

There is no hiding the fact that Sally was pro-Confederate, but she was a nurse first. She once stated that she would like to meet Clara Barton[27] to discuss nursing techniques, but she knew that would be impossible with Miss Barton being a "Yankee."

Even though suffering extreme shortages of supplies and medicines, Confederate hospitals in general often had a better survival rate than their Northern counterparts. This survival rate may partly have to do with maggot therapy which was used much more in the South. Maggot therapy involved the introduction of living, uninfected maggots into an open wound. The maggots would eat only the dead flesh and prevent gangrene from setting in. The treatment had been used to a very limited extent for centuries, but it was popularized during the Civil War by Joseph Jones, a ranking Confederate medical officer. He was quoted as saying:

> I have frequently seen neglected wounds ... filled with maggots ... as far as my experience extends, these worms eat only dead tissues, and do not injure specifically the well [sic] parts.[28]

There is no evidence that Sally used this therapy, but since its use is reported to have been widespread in the South, she must have at least known about it. Whatever her methods, news of her success in healing spread so quickly that wounded and sick soldiers begged to be sent to her.

The Confederate Government felt there was a great need for control of medical supplies, and they were not plentiful. The government was beginning to question the need for decentralized, private hospitals. Granted, there was some corruption in private hospitals in Richmond during the war. Indeed, some feared that some hospitals were harboring men who were not so sick but just really did not want to return to the war. Some private hospitals overcharged the Confederate government for their services. This overcharging problem would not have applied to the Robertson Hospitals since Sally financed the hospital herself and through donations.

In September 1861, only a few weeks after Robertson Hospital opened, Confederate President Davis issued an executive order to standardize all hospitals under the military hospital system and military rule. The order also stated that all hospital directors must at least hold the rank of Captain.

The order would result in the closing of all private hospitals and the removal of all the soldiers to public hospitals. The intent of the Confederate government was to reduce the number of hospitals and end the corruption. In effect, the order said that a woman could not run a hospital and Sally's hospital was slated for closure.

President Jefferson Davis was not the kind of person who would revoke a Presidential order, but he had not yet met Sally Tompkins. When Sally first heard of this order she cried, but she was not the kind of person who would take no for an answer.[29] Again, Sally had connections.

One of Sally's cousins was Judge William W. Crump who happened to be the Assistant Treasury Secretary of the Confederacy.[30] She begged him to help her get an audience with President Davis. She wanted only the opportunity to present her case to Davis for keeping Robertson Hospital open. Judge Crump persuaded Sally to accompany him to the personal office of President Davis to make her direct appeal.[31]

When they arrived at President Davis' office, he appeared dignified but very remote.[32] The President's office itself was a little intimidating. Davis told Sally that he had heard of her hospital and seemed impressed with the fact that she financed it herself. He knew why she had come and said to her that he could not ignore government regulations.[33]

Sally brought along her hospital register[34] that clearly illustrated the hospital's amazing success rate and how quickly her patients were returned to their military duties. In a firm voice, she presented her case why Robertson Hospital should not be closed.

Davis paused for a moment, then paced the floor for a few moments more. He then stared out a large window at a magnolia tree. In the meantime, Sally was moving her lips as if in prayer. Suddenly President Davis turned with an uncharacteristic smile and said "Miss Tompkins we will make you an officer in the Army of the Confederacy. You'll be under government jurisdiction, and thus your hospital will be saved."[35]

This was one of the few times anyone had ever seen Sally smile. She accepted the commission but told Davis that she would refuse any pay. She entered President Davis' office that day as Miss Sally and departed as Captain Sally Louisa Tompkins, Confederate Cavalry.

Confederate States of America,
WAR DEPARTMENT.
Richmond *Sep'r 9th* 1861.

Sir:

You are hereby informed that the President has appointed you

Captain

IN THE ARMY OF THE CONFEDERATE STATES. You are requested to signify your acceptance or non-acceptance of said appointment: and should you accept you will sign before a magistrate, the oath of office herewith, and forward the same with your letter of acceptance to this Department.

L. P. Walker
Secretary of War.

Cap'n Sally Tompkins
Richmond
Va

I accepted the above Commission as Captain in the C.S.A. when it was issued. But I would not allow my name to be placed upon the pay roll of the army.

Sally L. Tompkins

Captain Sally Louisa Tompkins' Commission
The American Civil War Museum,
under the management of
The Virginia Museum of History and Culture

CHAPTER 5

Captain Sally's Hospital

What was officially named the "Robertson Hospital" soon began to be called "Captain Sally's Hospital," although she would hear of no other name for it than "Robertson."[36] It was certainly her hospital though, and she ran it like a Prussian drill sergeant.[37] Out of the 1,334 patients she served during the War, she outranked all but four (two majors and two colonels). She was even sometimes addressed as "Sir."[38]

A Corporal Abner Jenkins, Jr. wrote home to his mother about the conditions at Sally's Hospital:

Dear Ma,

After them [sic] long weeks of bullets and beans, I'm sure eating good, Instead of hardtack, it's jellies and custards, chicken and stews; and I'm resting in a clean bed too. There's a powerful lot of scrubbing and washing here, my beard is done shaved, my hair cut neat, and clean drawers every morning. I ain't been this pure since the day I was born. At bedtime Miss Sally calls us to kneel, even though some got to handle a crutch, We call her "the little lady with the milk-white hands." Ma, you'd be glad the way she prays and reads us the Word.

Your loving son,
Abner Jenkins, Jr.[39]

In another letter (probably not to his mother) from the same Corporal Jenkins, he tells a slightly different story. Here he learns a lesson in rank:

> I done got permission to stroll out to town. Had me a whore and a quart of good whiskey. When I finally found my way back to Robertson's that little lady done [sic] jumped on me. Then she made me kneel and pray, plumb took all my clothes away. This morning I had me a hell of a headache. My clothes locked up, I stayed in bed. I asked the Captain's pardon – that lady ranks me.[40]

Private Jenkins apologized to Captain Sally and promised that he would never repeat his misdeed. Captain Sally returned his clothes to him.[41]

Captain Sally worked exhaustively each day from dawn to dusk. She ruled her hospital with a Bible in one hand and a stick in the other and with her medical kit attached to her belt. She even went to bed with her medicine chest still strapped to her side and her bible in her hand.[42] Her patients learned not to argue with her. She was a devout woman, and the discipline at the hospital was rigid. But the men still adored her, even when she scolded them.

There were no military guards at the hospital. The staff had to sometimes restrain the patients themselves. Sometimes they got help from the same patients. Once, in his delirium, a patient struck one of the nurses as she attempted to administer his medicine. A North Carolinian soldier, suffering from typhoid fever but with true Southern gallantry, sprang from his cot and declared "No man shall ever strike a woman in my presence."[43] On another occasion, two of the hospital's female nurses left in a huff when an irreverent patient called them "spry old larks." It was Dr. A.Y.P. Garnett that lured them back.[44]

The men were well fed at the hospital, much better than they received while fighting. Whenever one of her patients was discharged from Sally's care, he received a knapsack or a blanket roll filled with clean durable clothing, a prayer book and a copy of the Gospels bound in oil-cloth. He also received warm socks knitting by Sally herself and left with a full stomach.

The hospital had been open only a few months when it received a celebrated guest. She was Mary Chesnut[45] whose husband had been a United States Senator from South Carolina before the war and became a Confederate officer. She, like Sally, also had connections in high places. Mrs. Chesnut wrote of this visit, "Went to Miss Tompkins's hospital. There I was rebuked. I deserved it."[46]

Sometimes states' rights worked against the Confederacy. It was common practice for hospitals in Virginia to serve the Virginian sick and wounded first. This was not true of Captain Sally's hospital. When Mary Chesnut marched in rather grandly and asked "Are there any Carolinians here?" Sally responded, "I never ask where the sick and wounded come from." Sally, however, was once a Mathews County native with ties to Gloucester County herself. She once stated, "My hospital can never be too crowded for a Mathews or Gloucester County soldier."[47]

Mary noted both the good and the bad:

> The men under Miss Sally's kind care look so clean and comfortable. Cheerful, one might say. They were pleasant and nice to see. One, however, was dismal in tone and aspect, and he repeated at intervals, with no change of words, in a forlorn monotone. "What a hard time we have had since we left home." But nobody seemed to heed his wailing. And it did not impair his appetite.[48]

Mary and Sally became friends, and Mary visited the hospital many times, often helping out with the nursing when she could. They would sometimes share watermelon together in Sally's private office.[49]

One nurse, Martha Carter of Georgia, was so strikingly beautiful that the wounded men could not stop looking at her. She was becoming a distraction. Sally once joked to her, "If you could only leave your beauty at the door and bring in your goodness and faculty."[50]

Work at the hospital certainly was not all eating watermelon and making jokes. Sally lost her first patient, Lieutenant A. B. Bird from a Texas regiment, in November 1861.[51] He would be the first of 73 to die on Sally's watch. Of 1,334 patients, 73 deaths is a remarkable record. Mary Chesnut wrote of her difficult time at the hospital:

> A boy from home has sent for me. He was lying on a cot, ill of fever. Next to him a man died of convulsions while we stood there. I was making arrangements with a nurse, hiring him to take care of this lad. I do not remember anymore, for I fainted.[52]

With each major battle, thousands of wounded would pour into Richmond. Dealing with almost constant death was part of the job description for hospital work. One unexpected death in 1862 hit Sally hard. Her slave and lifelong companion Phoebe died.[53] The relationship of a slaveholder and a slave was sometimes a very complicated one and not easily understood with 21st century sensibilities. Sally addressed her as "Mammy" and Phoebe had watched over her all her life. Sally grieved her loss as if she was a true family member, which in some ways she was.

Captain Sally's saddest duty was to write farewell letters for dying soldiers. One such patient was a soldier who had lost both legs and his sight. His name was Lieutenant Phillippe Broussard from Louisiana. He was only twenty-one years old and a casualty of the Battle of Gettysburg. Sally wrote as Phillipe dictates:

Dear Mother, Father, darling bride,

I feel my strength leaving, but I need to share these final thoughts. Missy, sweetheart, through sheets of pain I search for your dear body, now forever lost to me. I don't want to let go. How does my dying make us free? If you should ask how I died, and are told "at peace," it would be a monstrous lie. For the beloved South, I fought, lost two legs and my good sight. Now I question why, Why? I cannot help but despise what causes such maddening pain. Christ, what's all the killing for?

Phillipe[54]

Lieutenant Phillipe Broussard died violently, not peacefully. His last words were: "Mama, Papa, Missy, weep, weep for me."[55]

One of the saddest stories of all was of a young fourteen-year-old boy named Nathaniel Newman who had run away from his Georgia home to follow his father into war. His father, Captain Newman, brought his sick son to Captain Sally's hospital, where the hospital found that Nathaniel was suffering from Tuberculosis. Sally made the boy as comfortable as possible and called in a Reverend to baptize the boy. Soon after, young Nathaniel died. The whole hospital was overcome with grief.[56]

THE ROBERTSON HOSPITAL, RICHMOND, VIRGINIA
Established by Capt. Sally Tompkins, 1862

Robertson Hospital 1865
The Library of Virginia

CHAPTER 6

The Lady in Charge

The blockades and the war were causing items to be very hard to obtain and incredibly expensive. There were bread riots in Richmond as food became harder to find. Partly because Robertson Hospital had its own garden, and partly because of contributions from friends of Sally, the patients at her hospital always got enough to eat. There is no known record of her hospital ever being bothered by the rioters.

One frequent visitor to the hospital (but mindful of the shortages) was Colonel Walter Taylor[57] who was also an aide to General Robert E. Lee. Walter had known Sally when she was a student in Norfolk and lived only a few blocks away. He was apparently quite fond of her although engaged to a Miss Bettie Saunders of Richmond. Walter seemed to like Sally's hospital food and sometimes ate with her in her private office at the hospital. Understanding the food shortages that plagued Richmond, he would pay Sally generously for the food. He wrote to his sister, "[I] take nothing from Sally. We should not & cannot use what her patients require."[58] In another letter, he goes on about Sally for taking in two young girls to live with her, "Isn't this like the good lady? I declare she is an angel on earth – or I should say she is a true woman."[59]

One of Sally's many male admirers was a British gentleman by the name of Anthony Snowden, formerly of Her Majesty's Navy. He was at this time a blockade runner for the Confederacy and also seemed to be quite taken by Sally. Blockade runners were an essential part of supplying the hospital. Sally was happy to purchase what she needed from them. When Sally asked Captain Snowden "Can you help me, Captain Snowden?" He bent low to kiss her hand and called her "Dearest of Captains." He promised her all that she wished.[60]

A letter Sally received from her sister, Maria, in March 1863, underscored the hard times and Sally's dedication to the war effort. The letter also illustrated the contrast between the sisters' personalities and priorities.

Dear Sally,

I have written for so many things that were necessary to my comfort & which you have not noticed, that my heart fails me to write again, but I must make one more effort…There are servants here to whom I must give something and I have nothing less than a dollar note & it will take quite a fortune to give each a dollar. Please send me in a letter some halves and quarters if possible to give them. Now please do this at once.

My clothes are in a horrid condition. My chemises & stockings are literally falling off me… It has been several weeks since any of you wrote to me & I cannot imagine why I am so ignored. I asked you to send me a cake of soap & am now actually without any, & you may know a trial it is to me, whose happiness is easily disturbed by soiled fingers and nails.

I never expected to be brought to soiled fingernails, stocking with holes, & dresses rubbed out at the

elbows...Now please do not forget the purpose
of this scrawl; some notes of the value of halves
& quarters...You never tell me anything. I do not
realize that I have any relations in the world.

With love to all adieu
your sister Maria.[61]

Sally could not have known that her sister, Maria, would die
a little more than a year later. At the time, she had much bigger
fish to fry and little time to be catering to her sister's relatively
frivolous wants and needs. In the months before she received her
sister's letter, Sally was dealing with the whole spectrum of war-
related illnesses, injuries and wounds. One doctor wrote, "soldiers
appeared to have been wounded in every conceivable way."[62]

These illnesses included, to name only a few, pneumonia, fevers,
bronchitis, dysentery, hepatitis and what was then called "soldier's
heart" which is now called "post-traumatic stress disorder." Many,
if not most, of these illnesses were not very well understood at that
time. Some illnesses were so vaguely described that they would
seem very strange to a modern medical doctor, such as "thin-
blooded," "worn out," or just "badness." In addition to fighting all
these sicknesses, Sally was also busy fighting off more attempts to
shut down her hospital.

Captain Sally's single-minded commitment to her work was
often surrounded by controversy and with battles to keep the
hospital open. In addition to a lack of supplies, she still had to
deal with public criticism and male resentment. Sally had to
maintain a delicate balance between being a nonconventional
Lady hospital administrator and being a proper Southern lady
with all its traditional confines. She was not going to change for
the world. The world was going to have to change for her.

Confederate Inspector of Hospitals, William A. Carrington,
seemed to have it in for Sally. He directed all hospital correspondence
directly to the hospital's Chief Surgeon Dr. A.Y.P. Garnett, and he
would respond to the correspondence keeping Sally out of the

loop. In a letter to the Surgeon Medical Director E.S. Gaillard, Inspector Carrington even referred to Chief Surgeon Garnett as being the one "in charge" of the hospital.

When Sally heard of the letter's content she felt a sense of betrayal by her Chief Surgeon whose salary was being paid out of her own pocket. She was, as Dr. Garnett himself once put it, "*The Lady in Charge.*"

Inspector Carrington had been informed that the hospital was caring for forty-four patients when they had beds for only nineteen. He wrote to Dr. Garnett:

> You are directed to transfer 25 of the patients in Robertson without delay…and not receive into the Hos[pital] in future more than 19 – the number you were ordered by the Surgeon Genl. to receive. If such resolution of orders and disregard for the safety of the sick and wounded occurs again the Hospital will necessarily be closed as a nuisance.[63]

Dr. Garnett wrote back that the hospital had room for twenty-two patients and that he would reduce the number of patients to that number, but also mentioned that some patients were housed in private homes but under hospital care. The next day Carrington sent a letter to Dr. J. J. Gravatt, a surgeon at Richmond's General Hospital No. 9, directing him to send no more patients to Robertson Hospital.

When she got wind of this, Tompkins, secure in her rank, responded directly to Inspector Carrington in a letter with a slightly angry tone:

> Dr. Garnett endorsement on the morning report was written under a misapprehension of the facts. The number allowed (by measurement) was 22, but in consideration of the number of chambers, it was extended to 25. Dr. Garnett found on examination

that there were occupying beds in the hospital at that time but 22 patients. The remainder – entirely with his approbation, sleeping in private quarters, but fed and tended in this Hospital. Had Dr. Garnett but suggested that he considered the sick & wounded too much crowded, I certainly would have had them transferred to other hospitals...Dr. Garnett's numerous engagements have prevented his giving much time & attention to his patients of late – notwithstanding I think the register of this Hospital will show as a great success in its management of the sick and wounded as any other.[64]

Carrington revoked his order for the hospital's closure in a caustic letter to Dr. Garnett, admonishing him that nurses (i.e. Sally) "should confine themselves to duties assigned... and be under your authority...if anything in the orders relating to reports...are not executed, you alone will be considered responsible." Despite Inspector Carrington's determination to ignore Sally's role as the hospital manager, she continued to remain the lady in charge.

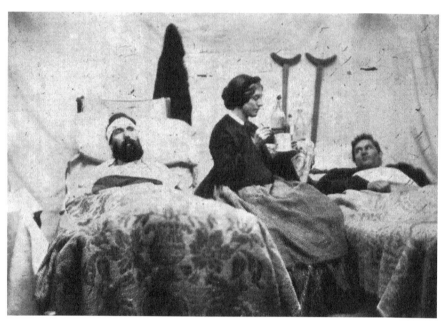

Civil War era hospital c. 1862

CHAPTER 7

The Last Days

Survival was difficult in the last years of the War. Scurvy and typhoid fever ran rapidly throughout the city. Nearly a foot of snow fell on Richmond in the spring of 1863. When the snow melted, the roads turned into mud making it difficult for farmers to carry their food into the city to sell. Everything was hard to come by. Food riots continued.

In spite of many, but costly, victories in the first two years of the War, the Confederate Army was beginning to lose steam. As battle after battle was fought, the flood of wounded into the city continued. The War was changing from a gentleman's war to a very bitter one. Resentment toward the North and Northern people was increasing.

The Union blockade of southern ports was becoming more and more effective with each passing day. In the last year of the War, Richmond was being protected by a series of entrenchments populated by poorly fed and maintained young boys and old men.

Most slaves in the south knew that a Southern defeat would be to their advantage. Many slaves in Richmond ran off to join the nearby Union troops. Many were just biding their time waiting for the inevitable. A puzzled Mary Chesnut once wrote in her diary, "why don't they all march over the border where they would be received with open arms."[65]

Sally paid her own slaves a handsome salary of $20 per month and "free men of color" $33. Her generosity may have been intended to keep them from running off and joining the Union Army since a "colored" Union soldier would make much less.

Sally's own slave, Peter Smith, was one who ran off late in the War. He returned very shortly after the War ended with apologies to Miss Sally, assuring her that his sole reason for leaving was to be free and was not because of her personally.

The end was certainly near. The Union Army broke through the Confederate lines at a place called Five Forks south of Petersburg, Virginia on April 1, 1865. The half-starved Confederates soldiers could put up only little resistance. Now, there was nothing in the Union Army's way between them and Richmond. What was left of the Confederate Army evacuated the Richmond area and marched west, hoping to link up with General Joseph Johnston's Army of Tennessee in North Carolina.

General Lee's aide Walter Taylor, who was so fond of eating Sally's food at the hospital, was one of the first to know of Gen. Lee's plan to evacuate Richmond. Still unmarried to his sweetheart "Bettie," he felt that a Confederate Officer's wife would have a better chance getting out of Richmond safely. He told Bettie that he wanted to get married to her immediately and explained why he thought it was necessary. She actually knew about Gen. Lee's plan to evacuate Richmond moments before Confederate President Davis himself knew. They were married on April 2, 1865 early in the morning. Sally loaned Walter a gold ring for his bride. The ring was from one of her cousins and was given to her for "safekeeping." She never got it back. Mrs. Walter "Bettie" Taylor said that she could not give up the ring which meant so much to her.

Before Col. and Mrs. Taylor and the Confederate troops evacuated Richmond, soldiers set fire to the city to keep it from being useful to the advancing Union troops. Even while much of the city was in flames, Robertson hospital admitted its very last patient. He was an artillery Sergeant named William B. Graves.

He was admitted because of a sprained ankle on April 2, 1865, as Union troops poured into the burning city. His minor injury probably did not require a hospital stay, but many years later he wrote to Sally saying that he wanted only to be able to tell his children and grandchildren that he had been a patient of Captain Sally.[66]

On the very same day, Sergeant Graves was admitted, Union General Godfrey Weitzel of the 25th Corps of the United States Colored Troops entered Richmond and accepted the city's surrender from the Mayor. Women and boys stood on the streets cheering and waving small Union flags.[67] The Union troops eventually managed to stop the raging fires, but about 25% of the city's buildings were destroyed.

President Abraham Lincoln, himself, arrived in Richmond on April 4, 1865, even as the city was still smoldering from the fires. He visited Jefferson Davis' home "The White House of The Confederacy" and also the former Confederate capital. He did not bother to visit Robertson's Hospital which was still in operation and only four blocks away. He may not have been too welcome anyway.

Only a few days later, General Lee's army found themselves surrounded at the town of Appomattox Court House. Lee was forced to surrender the remainder of the Confederate troops there on April 9, 1865. The terrible war was over and reconstruction would soon begin.

The last patient to die at Sally's hospital was John Crumley on April 10, 1865, just one day after the surrender. He had been a soldier but was employed by Sally as a gardener in the hospital after his gunshot wound in his right knee improved. Unfortunately, his wound had gotten infected, and he took a turn for the worst and died from the infection. He was originally from Ireland and people said that "he could coax vegetables from stones."[68]

Sally broke all regulations and did not release John Crumley's body to the occupying Union troops. She just refused to let the body fall into "Yankee" hands. After a week or so, Sally and "Glad" Betsy dressed him up in an ill-fitting, but clean, confederate uniform and Glad Betsy pinned a green ribbon on him. With the help of some of the hospital staff, they put Mr. Crumley's body in a cart and carried him through the ruins of Richmond to the Hollywood Cemetery to be laid to rest. He rests there still, by an old willow tree.

Lincoln was assassinated in Washington, D.C., only ten days after his visit to Richmond, by an actor named John Wilkes Booth. Booth broke his leg when he jumped from the president's box to the stage.

Booth thought that this killing would make him a hero in the south, but the opposite was true. The Southern people thought him a coward and very ungentlemanly to shoot an unarmed man from behind. Lincoln's death only brought more chaos to Richmond. John Wilkes Booth escaped, first by hiding out in the woods of Maryland then crossing the Potomac River. He headed south to the Rappahannock River where he crossed in a "horse boat." Due to strong currents, he missed the usual dock and landed on the "Riverview" estate of John Bernard Lightfoot. Lightfoot's wife was the former Harriet Ann Field, Sally Tompkins' second cousin and friend. Two of Harriet's daughters met Booth at the boat and saw that his leg was hurt. They offered to help him, but he declined their help saying that he "must be pressing on."[69] Had Booth accepted help from Sally's cousins, they may have been indicted for conspiracy to murder the President. Of course, they had no idea who Booth was and may not even have known about the assassination at that time.

Through all the chaos, Sally Tompkins continued to treat her patients at the hospital as if nothing had changed. The hospital finally closed its doors on June 13, 1865, two months after the Union forces occupied the former Confederate Capital.[70] There were no more patients to care for. A chapter in Sally Tompkins' life closed as well. Judge John Robertson and his family returned to Richmond to reclaim their house. Sally must have felt a combination of dread and relief.

Civil War Era Hospital Patients c. 1862

CHAPTER 8

Postwar Sally

With the close of Robertson Hospital, Sally Tompkins slipped into a period of relative obscurity, but she certainly was not forgotten by the former Confederate troops. For the rest of her life, she kept in touch with some of her former patients and continued to receive marriage proposals which she always declined. Postwar Sally apparently had no desire to open her own hospital, although she certainly could have. At age thirty-one years, she retired from the hospital business.

The city of Richmond, once a prosperous city, was now in dire straits. All banks and many businesses were destroyed in the fire. Nearly all cash was Confederate currency and was completely worthless. Federal authorities had to issue food rations to keep the people of Richmond from starving. Nothing would be the same as it was before the War, not for Sally and not for Richmond.

Sally Tompkins still found time to visit friends, but travel was not allowed in the reconstructed South without permission. Sally never traveled just for travel's sake but traveled when her nursing services were needed somewhere or to reconnect with family members. No one was more content to stay at home than she.[71]

In October 1865, Sally's seventeen-year-old second cousin, Emmeline [called Emmie] Allmand Crump, talked her into going with her on a trip to Gloucester and Mathews Counties. Emmie and her Aunt [Emmeline Madison Tabb Wellford] felt that Sally needed a diversion. Emmie's Aunt Emmeline felt that Sally suffered from what was then called the vapours[72] [depression] and that she needed "to put aside her grand and terrible memories of the war."[73] Their plan was to visit their relatives, the Tabb family at "Auburn" a farm near Poplar Grove. They were given permission to travel under the condition that they travel with an escort, Union Captain Benjamin Talbot plus about twenty U.S. cavalrymen and Union wagon drivers.

The trip somehow expanded into a caravan of four wagons. These were spring covered wagons with seats running sideways and each wagon was pulled by two horses.

The first wagon contained Emmie, her Aunt and her Aunt's sister-in-law, Miss Winnie Wellford. In the second wagon were Sally and her two young girl cousins, Annie and Ella Starke whom Sally had taken charge of after their mother died. Also in Sally's wagon was an unrelated man by the name of Mr. James, who lived in Gloucester and was just going along for the ride. A third wagon was carrying baggage and a fourth was filled with newly freed slaves. No one recording this event ever mentioned the African-American co-passengers, except to say they were there.

There are three accounts of this 80-mile journey. One is from Emmie's 1865 journal as the events were taking place. Another account was from a 1931 letter from an eighty-three-year-old Emmie (now Mrs. William B. Lightfoot) some sixty-six years later. A third account was from the writings of Captain Benjamin Talbot, the Union Officer in charge of escorting the parties to their chosen destinations. Interestingly, all three accounts pretty much report all events the same way, except for maybe who was flirting with whom. Emmie Crump wrote of the Captain in her Journal from October 1865:

> The cavalry officer in charge seems polite (I don't
> trust him.) He is sort of handsome, thick yellow hair

41

shiny as ripe wheat in the sun. I catch him ogling me with his brown eyes. I ignore him.[74]

However, Captain Talbot writes:

> I suppose these travelers are high-born Southerners, they snub me at every opportunity. Occasionally I catch the pretty young ladies casting glances under lashed in my direction...the one called Emmie... She is distractingly pretty with her tipped nose and golden curls...[75]

Captain Benjamin Talbot had no idea who Sally Tompkins was, and was puzzled why she was referred to as "Captain."

> The plain, stern looking one dressed in black is called "Captain,"...spends her time reading [probably the bible]... The grim lady Miss Tompkins...I think she's a sour old maid.[76]

The only Lady that ever talked to Captain Talbot was Mrs. Welford and that was seldom. Sally never even made eye contact with anyone, especially the Union cavalrymen. In Emmie's 1865 journal she always referred to them as DYs [Damn Yankees]. It can be safely said that the ladies on the trip and the Union cavalrymen did not get along.

The original plan for this traveling train of wagons was to travel by day and then camp at night along the way. After a heated argument between Captain Talbot and Emmie's Aunt Emmeline, they finally agreed that the ladies at least would stay the night at friends along the way. Emmie, her Aunt Emmeline, and her cousin Sally knew many people who lived along the way.

The first night they arrived at Aunt Emmeline's cousins the Jeffries in King and Queen County. Some of the union army drivers were nervous about approaching a Southern farmhouse so soon after the War. In Emmie's 1931 letter she writes:

I shall never forget the fear manifest by the Yankee driver when after a long argument between my aunt and the captain, he very reluctantly consented that we should go into the gate [of the Jeffries place] leading from the main road. The man evidently thought that danger lurked in every country road in Virginia, and naturally thought that the people would be hostile to those who had so recently despoiled their homes and property.[77]

They spent the night at the Jeffries home and left on their journey early the next morning. After they were many miles down the road, Emmie realized that she was missing a diamond ring her father had given her. She then remembered that she had left it on a washstand back at the Jeffries. She made such a fuss about it that Captain Talbot offered to send one of his men back to the Jeffries to retrieve the ring. Emmie refused his offer, writing in her 1865 journal, "I would not dream of trusting my precious ring to a DY."[78] The ring and owner were later reunited months later by a friend traveling to Richmond.

The second night was spent at the home of an Episcopal minister, Rev. Caraway who was also a friend of the Tabb family, then they left early the next morning. On the journey, everyone witnessed much poverty and destruction of farms caused by the War. The destruction only increased the animosity felt by the Virginians toward their Northern co-travelers.

The third evening they arrived at Gloucester Courthouse only to find the town occupied by intoxicated Union soldiers. Here Sally suddenly became animated and took charge. Captain Talbot noted in his journal that Sally was, "obviously accustomed to authority." Emmie writes:

Our third evening, we arrive at Gloucester Courthouse. To our disgust, the DY [Damn Yankee] soldiers stationed there are grossly inebriated...the

Captain and Aunt argue about where we should
lodge.

Cousin Sally, who has completely ignored all the DYs
[Damn Yankees] til now, takes charge, directs the
wagons to the home of her friends, the Taliaferros.[79]

It was not until the fourth day did Sally and friends arrive at
their chosen destination, the home of the Tabb family "Auburn."
Emmie continues in her 1865 writings:

Our Tabb cousins greet us and for the first time in
my life, I witness Sally weeping… [Cousin Ellen]
does not invite the DY [Damn Yankee] inside, has
Tansy [the housemaid] take him [Captain Talbot]
a tray – she reports his anger at not being asked
to come in the house. ..we [later] discovered a
vindictive message on, (of all strange places) Baby
William's wooden wagon. He expressed his anger
and contempt for our lack of hospitality…I wish he
hadn't been quite so handsome and, except for his
foolish note, he seemed in every way a gentleman.[80]

Captain Talbot was puzzled why the ladies seem to have such
animosity towards him since he had not participated in the War.
He was to express a slightly different take on the events of the trip:

Next morning…we arrive at a beautiful plantation…a
housemaid thrusts a tray in my hands; I'm startled
then enraged to be left under a tree with a tin plate
of cold cornbread and molasses…Childish though
it is, I feel insulted and cannot resist writing my
sentiments on a child's small wagon left outside.
I feel no malice toward these rebels, I'm puzzled
as to why they hold me in such low esteem. I spent
the War at Harvard [and] after graduation joined

a regiment sent to occupy Richmond. I've never harmed one Southerner.[81]

From her 1931 letter (sixty-six years later), Emmie had softened her feelings a little bit and pointed out how things have changed :

He [Captain Talbot] had taken this method of expressing his wrath and contempt for Virginia and its vaunted hospitality, called down the vengeance of Heaven upon Virginia and its people. We were only amazed and indignant that he should have expected to be entertained by a Virginia household, where hearts were so sore, fair lands lying waste and poverty to be experienced for the first time, and all on account of the actions of such as he. Now that same officer would no doubt receive a cordial welcome there, and receive the Virginia hospitality which is still as good as ever.[82]

Richmond, Virginia Shortly after the War

CHAPTER 9

The Captain was a Lady

After returning to Richmond from her trip to Mathews, Sally now turned her attention to a family matter. Her sister, Maria, who had died in July 1864 was buried in Norfolk, Virginia and Sally wanted her remains to be relocated and buried at their childhood home of Poplar Grove. The property was now owned by Judge Griffin Taylor Garnett, but the Tompkins family continued to maintain the family cemetery there, which was their legal right.

In December 1866, Sally wrote her half-brother (and only surviving sibling), Christopher, requesting a headstone for both Maria and her mother:

> Dear Bro C
>
> Ever since my return I have wanted to see you about removing the remains of my dear Maria but I have not been able to do so, once now I am afraid it is almost too late in the season for you to undertake it and I beg that you will not until <u>entirely</u> compatible to your <u>judgment</u> and <u>convenience</u>. I almost hesitate to call on you, but you so kindly offered your services that I ought not. I was (until I visited the graveyard

at Poplar Grove this summer) under the impression that there was a tombstone at my mother's grave. I remember perfectly making arrangements for one but I suppose the war prevented their completions so at the same time you get one for dear Maria I will be much obliged if you will get one for my mother too. I leave the selection of all <u>entirely</u> to your taste judgment having entire confidence in both. I have an idea what the expense of all will be which is one reason I have not spoken to you on this subject before. I have put aside $100 in gold for this purpose. Will you let me know if that will defray all expenses? I would not have you go to any expense whatever for I knew you have had great demands upon you. Whatever you do I will be perfectly satisfied with so don't consult me about anything.

Ever your devoted sister Sally[83]

Sally, being a devout Episcopalian, attended St. James' Church at Fifth and Marshall streets in Richmond. During the latter part of the 1860s and through much of the 1870s she became more active in the Church. She taught a Sunday school class and even contributed money, although her own fortune was nearly gone. The Church had become racially integrated after the War. One member was "Sad" Betsy who, although now free, stayed with Sally and became her cook.

Sometime after the war, Sally visited John Hopkins Hospital in Baltimore Maryland (Still below the Mason-Dixon line which she refused to cross). She was treated with great respect and asked to examine their record of typhoid fever patients, which she found showed a higher percentage of death than hers. To the inquiry as to what medicines she used she replied: "We had nothing but whiskey and turpentine."

Sally's half-brother, Christopher, died in 1877 at the age of sixty-four. Sally was now the only survivor of all the eight Tompkins children who once lived at Poplar Grove. It is fairly certain Sally's mind would sometimes drift back to a simpler time at Poplar Grove when it was a home full of playful children.

By the 1880s, however, she resumed her work as a fulltime healer, moving back and forth between Richmond, Norfolk, and Port Royal to care for an extended network of family and friends. The caregiving she performed in the postwar period was of the traditional type that southern women often provided for close family and friends. Nursing activities began to dominate her life once again, but not as a Hospital administrator. In 1881, she spent a large part of the summer caring for a young Richmond woman who was ill with typhoid fever, and she devoted part of the fall to attending to a sick mother and son.

Through much of the 1880s, her primary residence was "Riverview", a Greek revival home on the Rappahannock River at Port Royal, Virginia. In had been the home of her cousin and adopted sister Harriet who had died in 1871. She lived there with Harriet's husband John Lightfoot and his very large family. Sally was called upon to nurse the entire Lightfoot family through a series of protracted illnesses.[84] She was also active at the local church, St. Peters.

In October 1886 Tompkins was called to the bedside of Dr. John James Gravatt, the surgeon who worked at Richmond's General Hospital No. 9. He was the doctor who was once directed not to send any more patients to Robertson Hospital during Sally's battle with Confederate Inspector of Hospitals, William A. Carrington. In spite of the past Sally nursed him through his final illness. At this juncture in her life, her reputation as a healer might have been comparable to known male medical professionals. She writes:

> Our dear good doctor was ill nearly five weeks...I staid [sic] with him every day from 6 am till 11 or 12 pm towards the last I came home earlier at night... There is no physician near here now [Port Royal Virginia] that we have any confidence in. Since Dr. G. died I have staid [sic] & with Mrs. G. She is quick

sick & thinks I can prescribe for her...I will stay
with her every night and most of the day. There is
a great deal of sickness here – not any that can be
attributed to the climate – but old chronic cases &
old people & they think I can help them so I am
obliged to go and of course I am not only willing
but truly thankful to be of use – but my time is
occupied.[85]

The United Confederate Veterans held their annual rally in
Richmond on June 30 – July 3, 1886. Sally was a guest of honor.
She had sent invitations to all her patients and people who were
in some way associated with the hospital. She provided private
lodging for those who could not pay for hotel rooms by renting a
large house and asked many to bring their families. On the house
hung a large banner reading "Welcome, Veterans of Robertson's
Hospital."

Sally received many RSVPs, some stating that they would attend
and some stating that they could not. Some RSVPs proposed
marriage, some for a second time, all of which she declined.
Among the attendees was her very last patient, Sergeant William
B. Graves.

Regrets came from Captain Anthony Snowden, Sally's blockade
runner who probably coined the phrase "Our Dearest of Captains."
He writes:

Dearest of captains, I deeply regret I cannot be
there with you and your brave men; pressing affairs
keep me at home, and unfortunately I'm rather in
debt. I'll never forget outwitting the Yanks. It was
great sport outwitting the Yanks. It was great sport
for me, and a privilege to serve you. God bless,
Dearest of Captains.[86]

Her friend, Nannie Lee (Robert E. Lee's sister-in-law) who
wrote "but for many reasons I cannot leave home just now."

One very touching reply came from Corporal Al Jenkins, who accredited Captain Sally for turning him from a dirt-poor soldier to a respectable married man. He thanked her for reading him Scripture, and saving the soul of a "poor country boy."

At her own expense, Sally provided typical Virginian food. There was Smithfield hams, crab meat, fried chicken, collards, potato salad, cake, custards and pudding. She even displayed her old hospital register, in which her former patients delighted in finding their names.

To some at least, Captain Sally Tompkins was not to be forgotten. From time to time, her former patients would on occasion visit her for the rest of her days and usually addressed her as "Captain Sally."

Captain Sally Tompkins c. 1910
The American Civil War Museum,
under the management of
the Virginia Museum of History and Culture

CHAPTER 10

Sally in Retirement

When her cousin's husband, John Lightfoot, moved his family to Richmond in 1886, Sally purchased his home in Port Royal, Virginia. She continued to travel back and forth to Richmond and Norfolk to nurse friends and family.

Although Sally's work as a healer placed a high premium on her time, she maintained her practice until the early years of the twentieth century. "I have hardly ever been more constantly occupied than this fall and winter." She began a Christmas Eve letter to her cousin Parke Bagby in 1888:

> Just now I am occupied with a poor old friend here who is the most destitute person you ever saw – she is almost, if not quite, 90 years old. Lives entirely alone....now the poor old thing has typhoid fever....I go to see her five and six times a day....& my last visit is about ten pm.[87]

A letter to Parke in February 1899 indicates the toll that the years of this work was taking on Sally's health:

Ever since I left dear Richmond Nov. 1st I have wanted to write to you, & especially at Christmas, … but writing is not as easy to one sixty-five as it was and where there is sickness I am usually in that room.[88]

Sally Tompkins seemed to always have a project to work on. There was one project in 1904 she wished she never had. In that year, the very church that her sister "Lizzie" helped restore in Mathews County, burned to the ground. This was particularly distressful to Sally. Her project was to rebuild it. She writes to her lifelong friend and financial advisor, Walter Herron:

University of Virginia
January 28, 1904

My Dear Walter

Have you heard what to me is real distress – that our dear little church – Christ Church – Kingston Parish Mathews County is <u>burned</u> to the ground except the brick walls – all in ashes! The church was used for service on the morning of Jan[uar]y the 17th the only time we have service there – then we have Sunday school and service and sermon – the minister then drives 6 miles on to another church for an afternoon service – this is the church my sister Lizzie built in 1839 with assistance from your father and other friends in Norfolk – it was only half mile from Poplar Grove - of course there is nothing in this world that interests me more as this dear little church. Sister Lizzie asked she might be buried in front of this church and have cut on her tombstone "O! Earth, Earth, Earth, hear the wind of the Lord." I have just received the last payment on the house I owned in Port Royal – one hundred dollars and twenty-one. I write to ask you to put the hundred dollars in bank for the rebuilding of the dear church – fix it – so if I die before it is used, the church will get it & I hope to add to it from time to time. I find this snowy day any paper is out so please excuse scraps – Please dear Walter let me know what my bank account is - $21. Please put to my acc[oun]t I hope John Saunders is better. I hope George, Hume & all are well. My love to Bettie and each member of your family. May God bless each of your households. Ever your devoted Sally.[89]

As the Church was being rebuilt, Sally's own health began to decline. She was someone who had always taken care of others and now needed to be taken care of herself. By 1906 her fortune was nearly depleted from her nursing activities.

The Confederate Women's Home, on Grace Street in Richmond, invited Sally to live there as an honored guest. The home had been established by the Commonwealth of Virginia in 1898 to provide care for needy female relatives of Confederate officers for the rest of their lives. Sally fell into a unique category. She was not a relative of a Confederate officer. She _was_ one.

Sally moved into the best room in the home. It is unknown what became of her cook "Sad" Betsy Curtis. In 1907 she felt that it was time to write her will. Sally especially wanted to leave some money to the Home that had been so kind to her. She writes to her friend Walter for help:

April 12th 1907
No 3 East Grace Street
Richmond, Va.

My dear Walter

I have just read your letter – I hoped you would be able to come, and watched the clock until time for the train to leave – My dear Walter what could I do without you! No one in this world could or would help me as you – I become much concerned about not fixing my will so as to leave a sum to this institution, the managers of this Home have given me the best room in the house – they have taken me as their guest and in every way been kind, considerate & liberal, I am anxious to show some appreciation of their kindness. I want to see you very much & if I can and the weather gets settled I will come down for a day or so. I will not write mine now. Will try to make a memorandum of what I wish done & send it to you so you can get Walter [his son] to write it out. God bless you now and ever is the earnest prayer of your ever devoted

Sally[90]

Although she had little money left at the end of her life, Sally Tompkins left money and personal artifacts for many friends and relatives. She also gave money to her church, to the Home for Needy Confederate Women, to Richmond's Sheltering Arms Hospital and to Memorial Hospital also in Richmond. She also asked to be buried next to her sister Elizabeth at Christ Church in Mathews County.

She was somewhat of a local celebrity in her later days. One might see Sally Tompkins maneuvering her way down a Richmond street or entering a store in Richmond and overhear someone say, "There goes Sally Tompkins!" Once Sally fell in the street, as elderly women sometimes do, but when it happened to Sally the incident was mentioned in the Richmond newspaper.

Sally Tompkins became very ill in June of 1916. The Richmond newspaper reported:

Although she was reported to be resting fairly comfortably at the Home for Needy Confederate

Women, doctors in attendance upon Captain Sally Tompkins, C.S.A. say that her changes of recovery are very slim. She is 80 [actually 83] years old and is suffering from the effects of an attack of acute indigestion which affected her heart.[91]

A few weeks later she died surrounded by her many nephews and nieces. The newspaper reported the sad news, this time using her title:

Captain Sally Tompkins, 83 years old, died yesterday of chronic nephritis at 8:45 o'clock in the morning, in the Home for Confederate Women. The funeral, with full military honors, will take place in Mathews County in the graveyard of the church which her sister Miss Elizabeth Tompkins, helped to establish in 1841.[92]

Newspapers all over the country, North, West, East and South, carried the news of her passing, many with a brief biography. Everyone in Richmond seemed sad and distressed. The Richmond paper the story front page coverage with stories and editorials.

Confederate veterans from all over the South attended Tompkins' funeral and accompanied her body to its final resting place in Mathews County. Tompkins' tiny coffin was draped with the Confederate colors in accordance with the custom observed at all funerals of Confederate officers. She was laid to rest at Christ Church cemetery with her sister Elizabeth, as she had requested. An eight-foot monument of white Virginia granite stands at the head of her grave, where to this very day, people leave flowers at her grave. The inscription reads:

Captain Sally Louisa Tompkins, C.S.A.
Born at Poplar Grove, Mathews Co., Va., Nov. 9, 1833
Died Richmond, Va., July 25, 1916
In grateful appreciation of her

services in maintaining the Robertson
Hospital at Richmond, Va. from 1861
to 1865, where 1300 soldiers were
tenderly cared for, this memorial
is erected by the Confederate
veterans and the United Daughters of
the Confederacy. President Jefferson
Davis gave her a commission as Captain
of Cavalry, unassigned, in order that,
because of its valuable work
in restoring so many men to the army,
this hospital should be under supervision.[93]

Dr. Beverley Dandridge Tucker, the second bishop of the Episcopal Diocese of Southern Virginia and an accomplished poet wrote a touching tribute shortly after Sally Tompkins' death in 1916:

Captain Sally Tompkins, C.S.A.

The clock hath struck! A life hath paid the cost.
The Captain now is dead: the one who stayed
The scythe of death, and who on others laid
The hand of life, hath now the river crossed.
This woman soldier of the cause that's lost
Amongst her country's wounded nursed and prayed;
For four whole years of war her rounds she made
And gave her wealth, her all, where needed most.

Oh South! Thy sons can ne'er a debt of love
Forget nor pay, except with grateful heart,
A gentlewoman of this noble stamp
Whose life reflects its glory from above:
"We pass this way but once, 'and ere we part
We know she joins 'The Lady with the Lamp.'"[94]

Proposed (and rejected) Statue of Sally Louisa
Tompkins designed by Salvador Dali.
Sketch is by Bill Wynne. The American Civil War Museum,
under the management of the Virginia
Museum of History and Culture

CHAPTER 11

Sally's Memorial

The story of how Richmond chose to honor Sally Tompkins is as complicated as her life story itself. There have been many attempts to honor Sally Tompkins for over one hundred years. Nearly all have had some opposition, as did Sally herself. In life, Sally received her opposition for being a lady. In death, her memorials received opposition for being a Confederate.

In very many ways Sally was more of a Confederate after the War than during it. She was completely unreconstructed. Friends and neighbors recalled that they had to carry her mail for her all over town because she would not use a Yankee stamp. She would not drink "Yankee" coffee and not patronize establishments that served it. Sally Tompkins' great-niece, Nellie Tompkins, remembered that she "remained a Confederate always." "Once when we were children, we were excited about going to New York City," Nellie Tompkins recalled. "She asked us why we would have any desire to cross the Mason-Dixon Line."

In spite of her Confederate leanings, helping the sick and wounded was her first priority. In a 1907 interview with the *Richmond Times-Dispatch* Sally said:

My aim and object was to help all I could, not be paid for it. What I did for the wounded and ill Confederate soldiers was entirely a work of love; I never took any pay — never.

The first attempt to honor Miss Sally was in her own lifetime on December 13, 1910. At age seventy-seven years, she unveiled a granite tablet marking the former site of the old Robertson Hospital. Her second cousin, John B. Lightfoot spoke at the dedication:

> …with great pleasure, I present to you Captain Sally L. Tompkins, of the Confederate States Army, and request that she unveil the slab that we have placed on this site, that posterity may come and see where stood her Robertson Hospital.[95]

Today the Third Street Diner occupies the spot at Third and Main where Robertson Hospital once stood. High on a brick wall outside the building that now houses a diner, the plaque is still there. It notes that on that site stood Robertson Hospital "in charge of Captain Sally L. Tompkins C.S.A."

By 1923, there was a movement by some remaining Confederate veterans to erect a monument to Captain Tompkins with the aid of some "Sally Tompkins" Chapters of the Daughters of the Confederacy.

It was not until June 3, 1925,[96] nine years after her death, that the granite monument at her grave was put into place. It was unveiled by John Warren Cooke and bears the following simple inscription:

> I was hungered and ye gave me meat.
> I was thirsty and ye gave me drink.
> I was sick and ye visited me.[97]

During World War II there was a critical shortage of competent nurses in the military. To help solve the crises, the United Daughters of Confederacy offered a Sally Tompkins Nursing scholarship to female lineal descendants of Confederate soldiers who were interested in becoming nurses.

When Sally died in 1916, she left $1000 from her dwindling estate to the Medical College of Virginia (now part of Virginia Commonwealth University). In 1950, the college administration recommended renaming the Medical College library in recognition of members of prominent Virginia families. The approved name was the "Tompkins-McCaw Library."

A stained-glass window memorializing Tompkins was dedicated at St. James's Episcopal Church in September 1961. The window was unveiled by a great-great-granddaughter of Judge John Robertson, who had donated use of his home for the hospital.

One of Richmond's odder "Tribute to Sally Tompkins" episodes occurred in 1966, when a Richmond committee approached Spanish painter Salvador Dali about creating a statue of her that would join the stately statues on Monument Avenue. Dali was known for surreal paintings such as *The Persistence of Memory* (the one with the melted clocks).

Dali's unrealized vision was for a statue featuring a likeness of Tompkins atop a twenty-foot-tall pedestal of Dali's little finger. The idea was that Tompkins would have been depicted as sort of a Saint George figure, holding a sword above her head while fighting the "dragon" of disease. It was widely believed, by everyone involved, that the style of statue would not fit well on Monument Avenue in Richmond, Virginia. It was rejected. The statue to Captain Sally Tompkins project on Monument Avenue was put on the back burner and never revisited.

The Tompkins Cottage in Mathews County, Virginia is a museum and also the headquarters of the Mathews County Historical Society since 1969. The building was once owned by Sally's father Christopher Tompkins and has been dated to about 1820. In the cabin is a small room dedicated to the memory of Sally Tompkins. Her coat and bed are on display there.

In the early 1980s, women veterans began pressing for a memorial to women in the U.S. armed services. Congress approved the Women in Military Service for America Memorial (WIMSA) in 1988.

Two years of fund-raising and design revision followed. A revised preliminary design was approved in July 1992, and the final design in March 1995. Ground was broken for the memorial in June 1995, and the structure dedicated on October 18, 1997. The memorial is at the entrance to the Arlington National Cemetery. The heart of the Memorial is the Register, an interactive database that includes the name, picture, service history and awards and decorations of nearly 245,000 past and present servicewomen, who have taken their rightful place in history for generations to come by registering their service with the Memorial. All these brave women mentioned in the register had served in the U.S. Military in some capacity but one, Captain Sally Louisa Tompkins, C.S.A.

In 2013 The Commonwealth of Virginia approved the construction of a monument for the Capital Square grounds including bronze statues of twelve women from four hundred years of Virginia history. Sally Louisa Tompkins was one of the twelve.

The controversy started almost immediately. Many people in Virginia wanted "no more new Confederate monuments." Following the violent white nationalist rally in Charlottesville, Virginia in August 2017 the controversy became more heated.

Virginia Governor Northam said Confederate current monuments "should be taken down and moved into museums." He said that he would "be a vocal advocate for that approach and work with localities on the issue." About two months later, during a forum at the University of Richmond, Governor Northam said he is "not going to meddle" in the decisions of localities and universities regarding Confederate statues.

Governor Northam appeared to see a distinction between Tompkins and other Confederate officers. "The governor… recognizes that the women who were selected for this monument contributed to Virginia at different times in our history and in different ways," said Northam's press secretary. "We should continue the conversation about monuments that were erected expressly to glorify individuals who fought a war against their own country to protect the institution of slavery, but we should also be honest about the difference between that and the recognition of a woman who only accepted her commission when it was the only way to keep her hospital open."

Former state Senator Mary Margaret Whipple stated "Tompkins was not chosen for her service to the Confederacy but for her work in service of saving people's lives…Tompkins was so respectful of hygiene that her hospital is said to have had the highest survival rate of any other."

Other people had different views. Chelsea Higgs Wise, assistant secretary of the Richmond Branch NAACP, believes it is inappropriate to include a statue of Tompkins. "We're not honoring losers anymore. And I understand that she has a great record as a medical professional, but they still lost," she said. "At the end of the day, if you were fighting for the Confederacy you were fighting for black people to be kept as slaves…How can we honor slaves and people that were fighting to keep people as slaves right beside them?"

State Senator Jennifer L. McClellan, chairwoman of the state's Dr. Martin Luther King Jr. Memorial Commission, has a different view. She said that her initial impression is that she does not have a problem with a statue of Tompkins. "I think she's a little different from Jefferson Davis and Civil War generals," McClellan said, adding: "I don't think being commissioned by the Confederacy undoes the good work she did to save lives."

Governor Ralph Northam will take part in the October 2019 dedication of the Virginia Women's Monument on Capitol Square, which is to include a statue of the Confederate captain. Sally Tompkins' statue will not be put up on a pedestal. It will be at ground level. Tompkins' brief biography in the event's program will note her pioneering achievements at Robertson Hospital, but not mention the Confederacy.

If this saintly-lifesaving woman had a dark side it would be her acceptance of slavery. It is difficult to enter the minds of her and her family about this complicated issue. We know that her sister, Lizzie, with good intentions, believed that all slaves should be freed and then relocated to Africa. The flaw in this logic would be that if they were free, then they should at least have the option to stay in America if they wished.

By all accounts, Sally was generous to her slaves, she even once hired an attorney to defend one of her slaves named William who was accused of stealing.[98] Of course, her generosity is beside the point.

One might argue that nineteenth century values are much different than twenty-first century ones or that at least some slaveholders were more ignorant than evil. Sally grew up on a large estate where at that time it would have been difficult for her to even imagine being operated without slave labor. Sally's cousin, Emmie, writing in a tone of sadness about "their inability to keep it up [the farm] without the labor they had been accustomed to," seems almost laughable today.

Many people of Sally Tompkins's wealth and status chose to move out of the country, to Europe or Canada, to sit out the War. Sally Tompkins did not. She stayed in the thick of it and spent her fortune to save lives.

William Shakespeare once wrote, "The evil that men do is remembered after their deaths, but the good is often buried with them."[99] Sally Tompkins certainly reversed that equation.

EPILOGUE

In 1980 Sally Tompkins was again in the news. A wealthy English gentleman, living in New York, bought her childhood home Poplar Grove in Mathews County, Virginia. He had told the people at Pentacles Realty, Inc., that he wanted a mansion with poles out front [he meant columns]. He wanted a tax shelter or perhaps to use the house as a recording studio. One can only imagine what he and his wife thought when they drove up to the house in their Rolls Royce.

The wealthy English gentleman's name was John Lennon and he was a former member of a rock band called the Beatles, (so his credit was good). Lennon was quoted saying:

> I heard how a girl named Sally was born there, grew up to be a nurse in the Yanks' Civil War' how all the wounded chaps fell for her.[100]

John, and his wife Yoko, spent the first night there, but it was too quiet for them. They occasionally spent other nights there. The couple had a caretaker at Poplar Grove, a Norwegian named Oggie, and they would visit from time-to-time to get away from the hustle of the big city.

Lennon owned Poplar Grove for less than a year before a deranged fan shot him outside of his New York City apartment. Yoko donated the plantation to charity, a nearby boys' home for abused children. Sally might have liked that.

APPENDIX 1

Sally Tompkins' Memorandum[101]

Having made my will disposing of all my estates, except certain personal effects, I now desire to dispose of these, and also to give certain directions for the disposition of my remains. I, therefore, direct as follows:

First: I wish to be buried in the same grave with my sister, Elizabeth, in the Church Yard at Christ Church, Kingston Parish, Mathews County, Virginia.

Second: I wish my sister Elizabeth's grave to be put in good order.

Third: To my cousins, Mrs. Ellen Tabb Lane and Kate Robertson, who have ever been as own sisters to me, I give all my personal effects which shall be at "Woodstock," Mathews County, as the time of my death, except my silver spoons, which I dispose of hereinafter.

Fourth: To the same Ellen and Kate I give, to the first, my black silk skirt, and to the second, my astrakhan cape.

Fifth: I give to Sally Braxton my work stand that was my sister Elizabeth's.

Sixth: To my niece, Ellen Wise, I give my silver sugar dish and cream pot, now in my room in Richmond.

Seventh: I desire that my silver spoons, now at Woodstock, in Mathews County, be sold and the proceeds to be devoted to the purchase of a <u>simple</u> Communion service for Christ Church, in Mathews Co., and, should such proceeds be insufficient to purchase such a set as the vestry of the Church may desire, then such vestry may add to such proceeds a sum to be taken from the money I have left said Church, sufficient for the purpose.

Eighth: To Mollie Lightfoot and Emmy Lightfoot I give the bureau and wardrobe now at Harriet Cringans. [Author's note: the Emmy stated here always spelled her name, Emmie.]

Ninth: To Howell Brooke, with a desire that he shall obey the injunction engraved within its case, I leave my gold watch. [Author's note: engraving reads "Redeem Time"][102]

Tenth: Any and all of my personal effects of which I may have made no mention herein, I desire Hal Brooke, Mollie Lightfoot, and Emmy Lightfoot to take charge of and make such disposition of them as they may see fit.

Eleventh: I wish my dear friends, Hal Brooke, Emmy Lightfoot and Mollie Lightfoot, to see that my wishes are carried out as herein expressed, and direct that none of the articles herein mentioned be apprised. It is my further desire that this memorandum, disposing of my effects as set forth be met probated as a part of my will.

In witness whereof I hereunto subscribe my name and affix my seal to this memorandum, the 15 th, day of April, 1907, at Richmond, Virginia.

(Signed) Sally L. Tompkins. (Seal)

Charlotte Lee
Annie Jones

APPENDIX 2

Sally Tompkins' Last Will and Testament[103]

I, Sally L. Tompkins, of Richmond, Virginia, do make this my last will and testament, hereby revoking all former wills by me made.

Having made and signed a written memorandum, dated April 15th, 1907, giving directions as to the place of my burial, and as to the disposition of my personal effects, which is not to be probated as a part of this my will. I shall now dispose of my estate.

First: I direct that all my just debts be paid.

Second: I give and bequeath the sum of One Hundred and Fifty Dollars ($150.00), to each one of the following relations and friends:

Mrs. Ellen Tabb Lane, of Mathews County, Va.

Mrs. Kate H. Robertson, of Mathews, County, Va.

Mrs. Lydia Taylor, of Norfolk, Va.

Mrs. Harriet A. Brooke, of Richmond, Va.

Mrs. Emmeline Lightfoot, of Richmond, Va.

Mrs. Mollie B. Lightfoot, of Richmond, Va.

Mrs. Augusta A. Daniel, of Richmond, Va.

Dr. Christopher Tompkins, of Richmond, Va.

Col. Walter H. Taylor, of Norfolk, Va.

Third: I direct that my Executor, hereinafter named, shall invest the residue of my estate either in first mortgage real estate loans, or in such other safe securities as he may deem advisable, and pay ever the income therefrom to my niece, Clementine M. Tompkins, during her life.

Fourth: On the death of said Clementine M. Tompkins, I direct my Executor to pay the following legacies out of said residue:

To the Confederate Home for Needy Women, Richmond, Va., the sum of One Thousand Dollars ($1000).

To Christ Episcopal Church, Kingston Parish, Mathews County, Va., the sum of One Thousand Dollars ($1000).

To the Sheltering Arms Hospital, Richmond, Va., the sum of One Thousand Dollars ($1000).

To the Memorial Hospital, Richmond, Va. (to which I have heretofore given $100.00), the sum of Nine Hundred Dollars; providing the Board of Directors of said Hospital will call one of the patient's rooms "The Tomkins Memorial Room" after my father, Christopher Tompkins, and my mother, Maria Boothe Tompkins, and attach a brass plate to the door or wall of said room bearing the names of my said parents.

Fifth: Should there be any residue of my estate, after the payment of the legacies provided for in the Fourth clause of this will, or should any of said legacies lapse, then I give and bequeath one-half of said resides or lapsed legacy, to Mrs. Harriet A. Brooke; or, if she be then dead, to said Confederate Home for Needy Women; and I give and bequeath the other half to Mrs. Emmeline Lightfoot; or, if she be dead, to said Confederate Home for Needy Women.

Sixth: I appoint my young friend, Walter H. Taylor, son of R. C. Taylor, of Norfolk, Va., as my Executor; and request that no security be required of him as such Executor. [Author's Note: Walter would die a few months before Sally.]

Witness my hand hereto affixed this 7th, day of May 1907.

(Signed) Sally L. Tompkins

Signed and declared as and her last
will and testament by Sally L. Tompkins,

In the presence of us, who, in her presence and
In the presence of each other, have hereto subscribed our
Names as witnesses.

Charlotte Lee

Annie Jones

APPENDIX 3

Newspaper Article

Richmond Newspaper Article published weeks before her death[104]

Richmond, June 22, 1916

Anna M. D. Yeatman

Although she was reported to be resting fairly comfortably in the Home for Needy Confederate Women, doctors in attendance upon Captain Sally Tompkins, C.S.A. say that her chances of recovery are very slim. She is 80 [actually 83] years old and is suffering from the effects of an attack of acute indigestion which affected her heart.

Nearby the Home is the site of the Robertson Hospital of which Captain Tompkins had charge during the War between the States. A tablet on the side of the building which displaced the hospital years ago reads thus: "On this site stood the Robertson Hospital in charge of Captain Sally Tompkins, C.S.A. - from 1862 [actually 1861] to 1865 – Placed by the Confederate Memorial Literary Society.

In these days of organized philanthropic work, women can find easy outlet for their superfluous time and energy. We, who hesitate over the merits of various opportunities of self-dedication presented to us, rarely consider how much we owe to those who possessed insight to recognize their field of labor of their own initiative. Any detailed account of woman's work in this locality would be incomplete without reference to the labors of two well-beloved living women, both closely identified with Norfolk.

The first of these is Captain Sally Tompkins, the only female commissioned officer in the Confederacy. In the early [eighteen] sixties, the position of this young lady was unusual. Her ancestral home of "Poplar Grove" in Mathews County had been recently sold and many of the negroes of that estate had been legally freed and placed into life. Part of the family fortune had gone to the building of Christ Church, Mathews county. Miss Tompkins and her sister lived in Richmond with a large corps of house servants, who were too much part and parcel of their lives to be dispersed and who missed the activities of plantation life, Miss Tompkins saw her opportunity for a life-work and promptly embraced it. She placed herself and servants at the service of her country in the Robertson hospital in Richmond, which was supported by her private means. Medicine was contraband of war, and her treatment for all diseases was air, light, cleanliness, turpentine and whiskey (all home products) and quinine, when it could be run through the blockade lines. If these failed, her panacea was prayer and the bible. The percentage of her recoveries holds its own with the records of today's most scientific treatment. When her private fortune was spent, the War Office of the Confederacy bestowed upon her a captain's commission so that she could draw her supplies from the Commissary Department. This commission can be seen at the Confederate Museum [now the National Civil War Museum] in Richmond.

For many years after the war, Miss Tompkins was closely associated with Norfolk. Today she is one of the most beloved figures in Richmond, a little black-robed woman dependent on the love and sympathy of her friends. It was the writer's recent privilege to be with her in one of the department stores and her progress was dignified by the escort of department heads and the exclamations of the girls behind the counters: "There goes Miss Sally Tompkins, bless her heart!"

The Florence Nightingales and the Clara Bartons of life would have done their work had European wars been non-existent, but the world would have been poorer without knowledge of their efforts; periods of storm and stress bring their own compensation for inevitable suffering, in developing divine opportunities of individual growth.

ABOUT THE AUTHOR

Author Thomas T. Wiatt with statue of John
Lennon in San Jose, Costa Rica

Thomas T. Wiatt is a distant relative of Sally Tomkins. He was born in Savannah, Georgia and lives in Newport News, Virginia. He is a graduate of Virginia Tech in Blacksburg, Virginia and Thomas Nelson Community College in Hampton, Virginia. Tom is a retired Engineer from Newport News Shipbuilding. He is presently an award-winning volunteer at the Mariners Museum and Park in Newport News, where he is a tour guide and a library research assistant. Other than history and writing, his passions include music and world travel.

He is also author of *Rev. William E. Wiatt / The Life and Times of a Confederate Chaplain and Related Family stories*, a book about his great-great-grandfather.

BIOGRAPHY

1. The Clan of Tomkyns, 1957. An unfinished and unpublished book by Robert Angus Tompkins.
2. *the lady with the milk white hands: A Biography of Captain Sally Tompkins* by Shirley E. Gillespie, copyright 2005 Two Dogs Publishing.
3. Unpublished and undated manuscript by Blanche Chenery Perrin. (Circa 1960).
4. *Dearest of Captains, a biography of Sally Louisa Tompkins* by Keppel Hagerman. Brandylane Publishers, Copyright 1996.
5. *Mary Chesnut's Civil War* (1981).
6. *The Private Mary Chesnut, The Unpublished Civil War Diaries*, C. Vann Woodward and Elizabeth Muhlenfeld.
7. *The Descendants of Stephen Field of King and Queen County Virginia, 1721* by Alexander Lloyd Wiatt, Copyright. 1992.
8. *A Diary From Dixie*, A woman's Journal of the Civil War, copyright 2011.
9. *Virginia Women* Their lives and Times – Volume 1, edited by Cynthia A. Kierner and Sandra Gioia Treadway.
10. *Historic Homes and Properties of* Mathews County, Virginia Pre-Civil War, Mathews County Historical Society.

NOTES

1 Comparing her prewar photograph with her wartime one, one can see that she lost weight and the strain of the war probably took its toll on her appearance.

2 https://wc.rootsweb.ancestry.com/cgi-bin/igm.cgi?op=GET&db=bbarnhardt&id=I618

3 Land Plat Book I, p. 242-243., Mathews County, Virginia.

4 *Richmond Enquirer* obituary, Richmond, Va., 13 August 1824.

5 https://wc.rootsweb.ancestry.com/cgi-bin/igm.cgi?op=GET&db=bbarnhardt&id=I618

6 The Clan of Tomkyns, 1957. An unfinished and unpublished book by Robert Angus Tompkins.

7 His surviving children were Martha born in 1807, Harriet born in 1809, and Christopher born in 1813. His son Henry born in 1811 died at age three in 1814.

8 Letter written by Maria Booth Patterson to Harriet Field, dated December 25, 1837.

9 Richmond Whig & Public Advertiser", Richmond, VA, Tuesday, August 28, 1838.

10 The Diary of Dr. Henry Wythe Tabb.

11 *The Captain was a Lady*, Virginia Cavalcade, Vol VI, No. 1., Summer 1956.

12 Letter from twelve-year-old Sally Tompkins to her brother Christopher Q. Tompkins dated May 18, 1846. Sally's misspelled words were corrected in this for publication clarity purposes.

13 Unpublished and undated manuscript by Blanche Chenery Perrin. (Circa 1960). This source is considered historical fiction and may be unreliable.

14 *Captain Sally Louisa Tompkins, C.S.A.* by Gerald W. Morgan, Confederate Veteran, Vol. 5 2000.

15 1851 – 1852 Norfolk City directory.

16 Adam Foster to his daughter Cynthia, January 7, 1847, qtd. in Gillespie, *lady with the milk white hands*, page 33.

17 U.S. Bureau of the Census.

18 *Confederate Ladies of Richmond* by Susan Provost Beller, p. 11.

19 An inflammation of the pleura that is typically characterized by sudden onset, painful and difficult respiration, and exudation of fluid or fibrinous material into the pleural cavity.

20 *The lady with the milk white hands: A Biography of Captain Sally Tompkins* by Shirley E. Gillespie, copyright 2005 Two Dogs Publishing, page 15.

21 Unpublished and undated manuscript by Blanche Chenery Perrin. (Circa 1960's). This source is considered historical fiction and may be unreliable.

22 Letter from Sally Tompkins to Parke Bagby, dated June 7, 1892, Bagby family Papers, Virginia Historical Society.

23 *The lady with the milk white hands: A Biography of Captain Sally Tompkins* by Shirley E. Gillespie, copyright 2005 Two Dogs Publishing.

24 *Captain Sally Tompkins*: Angle of Mercy by Tommie LaCavera, Historian General, UDC Magazine March 1992, Vol LV #3 page 8

25 *The Captain was a Lady*, Virginia Cavalcade, Vol VI, No. 1., Summer 1956

26 Ibid.

27 Clara Barton was a pioneering nurse during the American Civil War who also founded the American Red Cross.

28 Donnelly, J (1998). "Wound healing – from poultices to maggots. (a short synopsis of wound healing throughout the ages)". "Wound healing--from poultices to maggots. (a short synopsis of wound healing throughout the ages)". *The Ulster medical journal*. 67 Supplement 1: 47–51.

29 *The Captain was a Lady*, Virginia Cavalcade, Vol VI, No. 1., Summer 1956

30 *The Evacuation of Richmond* by William B. Lightfoot, page 215

31 *The Captain was a Lady*, Virginia Cavalcade, Vol VI, No. 1., Summer 1956

32 *Dearest of Captains, a biography of Sally Louisa Tompkins* by Keppel Hagerman. Brandylane Publishers, Copyright 1996, Pages 29 and 30.

33 Ibid, page 29.

34 The Robertson Hospital Register is an 84-page handwritten logbook of Civil War patients admitted between August 3, 1861, and April 2, 1865. There are 1,329 entries in the register, each assigned a case number. 5 case numbers have no entries while number 866 was used twice. To see the information in the Robertson Hospital registrar, download this link: https://digital.library.vcu.edu/digital/collection/rhr/id/544/rec/172.

35 *Dearest of Captains, a biography of Sally Louisa Tompkins* by Keppel Hagerman. Brandylane Publishers, Copyright 1996, Page 30.

36 *The Captain was a Lady*, Virginia Cavalcade, Vol VI, No. 1., Summer 1956.
37 *Dearest of Captains, a biography of Sally Louisa Tompkins* by Keppel Hagerman. Brandylane Publishers, Copyright 1996.
38 *The Captain was a Lady*, Virginia Cavalcade, Vol. VI, No. 1., Summer 1956.
39 *Dearest of Captains, a biography of Sally Louisa Tompkins* by Keppel Hagerman. Brandylane Publishers, Copyright 1996.
40 Ibid., page 38.
41 *The Captain was a Lady*, Virginia Cavalcade, Vol. VI, No. 1., Summer 1956.
42 *Captain Sally*, submitted by Reed Alvord of Hamilton, New York to the *Civil War Times*, October 1998.
43 Anonymous, "'Captain' Sally Tompkins," *Confederate Veteran*, Volume 16 (1908), p. 72.
44 *The Captain was a Lady*, Virginia Cavalcade, Vol. VI, No. 1., Summer 1956.
45 *Mary Chesnut's Civil War* edited by C. Van Woodward; copyright 1981, a diary that won the Pulitzer Prize for History in 1982. Literary critics have praised Chesnut's diary as "a work of art" and a "masterpiece" of the genre. Unlike her husband, Mary Chesnut was opposed to slavery.
46 Ibid.
47 *The Captain was a Lady*, Virginia Cavalcade, Vol. VI, No. 1., Summer 1956.
48 *The Private Mary Chesnut, The Unpublished Civil War Diaries*, C. Vann Woodward and Elizabeth Muhlenfeld, page 140.
49 Ibid., pages 125 and 128.
50 *Mary Chesnut's Civil War* edited by C. Van Woodward; copyright 1981, page 149.
51 The Richmond Dispatch, November 26, 1861.
52 *Mary Chesnut's Civil War* edited by C. Van Woodward; copyright 1981, page 158.
53 *The Captain was a Lady*, Virginia Cavalcade, Vol VI, No. 1., Summer 1956.
54 Last letter home from Lieutenant Phillippe Broussard, 7th Infantry, Louisiana Regulars, dated September 1863.
55 *Dearest of Captains, a biography of Sally Louisa Tompkins* by Keppel Hagerman. Brandylane Publishers, Copyright 1996., page 50.
56 Lori Jackson Black, Paper entitled *Captain Sally Tompkins, CSA* 5/23/2016.
57 Late in the 19th century, Taylor was active in the development of the Ocean View area of Norfolk, Virginia.

58 *Lee's Adjutant, The Wartime Letters of Colonel Walter Herron Taylor, 1862 – 1855, May 8, 1863*

59 Ibid, August 1, 1863

60 Lori Jackson Black, Paper entitled *Captain Sally Tompkins, CSA* 5/23/2016., page 41.

61 Letter from Maria Mason Tompkins to Sally Louisa Tompkins, dated March 7, 1863. Sally Louisa Tompkins – Robertson Hospital Collection.

62 *The Professor and the Madman* / A Tale of Murder, Insanity, and the making of the Oxford English Dictionary. Simon Winchester. 1999.

63 Letter from William A. Carrington to A.Y.P. Garnett, June 6, 1864.

64 Letter from Sally Tompkins to William A. Carrington, June 9, 1864.

65 *A Diary From Dixie*, A woman's Journal of the Civil War, copyright 2011., page 74.

66 Ibid., page 40.

67 The Confederate Veteran, Vol 17, page 215.

68 *Dearest of Captains, a biography of Sally Louisa Tompkins* by Keppel Hagerman. Brandylane Publishers, Copyright 1996., page 56.

69 *The Descendants of Stephen Field of King and Queen County Virginia, 1721* by Alexander Lloyd Wiatt, Copyright. 1992.

70 *Captain Sally*, The Civil War Times, October 1998, by Reed Alvord.

71 *The Captain was a Lady*, Virginia Cavalcade, Vol VI, No. 1., Summer 1956.

72 In Victorian times the disease, Vapours, was ascribed primarily to women and thought to be caused by internal emanations (vapours) from the womb. It is believed by some in the modern medical profession that ladies' tight corsets could squeeze their internal organs, including the lungs, and could restrict breathing causing the wearer to feel faint and suffer "*the vapours*".

73 The Journal of Miss Emmie Crump, October 10, to 16, 1865, From *Dearest of Captains,* a biography of Sally Louisa Tompkins by Keppel Hagerman. Brandylane Publishers, Copyright 1996, page 65.

74 Ibid.

75 *Dearest of Captains, a biography of Sally Louisa Tompkins* by Keppel Hagerman. Brandylane Publishers, Copyright 1996., page 68.

76 Ibid., page 69.

77 Letter from Mrs. William B. Lightfoot to Mrs. Mary James Tabb, December 29, 1931.

78 The Journal of Miss Emmie Crump, October 10, to 16, 1865, From *Dearest of Captains,* a biography of Sally Louisa Tompkins by Keppel Hagerman. Brandylane Publishers, Copyright 1996.

79 Ibid.

80 Ibid.

81 *Dearest of Captains, a biography of Sally Louisa Tompkins* by Keppel Hagerman. Brandylane Publishers, Copyright 1996., page 69.

82 Letter from Mrs. William B. Lightfoot to Mrs. Mary James Tabb, December 29, 1931.

83 Letter from Sally L. Tompkins to Christopher Q. Tompkins, December 7, 1866.

84 Sally Tompkins to Parke Bagby, August 9 and November 19, 1881, November 13, 1886. Bagby Family Papers, Virginia Historical Society. Harriet Field Lightfoot was Sally's second cousin and this author's great-great-great-great Aunt.

85 Letter from Sally Tompkins to Parke Bagby, October 7, 1886. Bagby Family Papers, Virginia Historical Society.

86 *Dearest of Captains, a biography of Sally Louisa Tompkins* by Keppel Hagerman. Brandylane Publishers, Copyright 1996., page 76.

87 Letter from Sally Tompkins to Parke Bagby, December 24, 1888.

88 Letter from Sally Tompkins to Parke Bagby, February 7, 1889.

89 Letter from The Walter Herron Taylor papers, Norfolk City Library, Norfolk, Virginia.

90 Letter from Sally Tompkins to Walter H. Taylor, April 12, 1907. Norfolk, Virginia Library.

91 *Richmond Times-Dispatch* newspaper article June 16, 1916 by Anna M.D. Yeatman.

92 *Richmond Times-Dispatch* newspaper obituary July 26, 1916.

93 *Tombstones of Mathews County, Virginia 1711 – 1986*, pages 156-157.

94 *Confederate Verses,* by Dr. Beverley Dandridge Tucker, 1916.

95 *The Captain was a Lady*, Virginia Cavalcade, Vol VI, No. 1., Summer 1956.

96 Biographical Chronology received from the Mathews County Historical Society.

97 The Gospel of Matthew, King James version, Chapter 25 Verse 35.

98 Mabel Boardman, *Under the Red Cross Flag at Home and Abroad.* Page 75.

99 Julius Caesar by William Shakespeare, Act 3, Scene 2.

100 *Dearest of Captains, a biography of Sally Louisa Tompkins* by Keppel Hagerman. Brandylane Publishers, Copyright 1996., page 85.

101 From the Ann Tompkins Branes and Eleanor S. Brockenbrough Library, National Civil War Museum, Richmond, Virginia.

102 *Dearest of Captains, a biography of Sally Louisa Tompkins* by Keppel Hagerman. Brandylane Publishers, Copyright 1996., page 80.

103 From the Ann Tompkins Branes and Eleanor S. Brockenbrough Library, National Civil War Museum, Richmond, Virginia.

104 *The lady with the milk white hands: A Biography of Captain Sally Tompkins* by Shirley E. Gillespie, copyright 2005 Two Dogs Publishing., page 60.

Made in the USA
Las Vegas, NV
12 November 2022

59311730R00062